DIESTERWEGS
NEUSPRACHLICHE
BIBLIOTHEK

AF217848

Hanif Kureishi

The Black Album

adapted for the stage by the author

edited and annotated by Rudolph F. Rau

Diesterweg
westermann

A special thanks to Jatinder Verma, who directed the play in 2010,
for providing background information and explaining the use of slang in the play.
Jatinder Verma is Artistic Director of Tara Studio – 356 Garratt Lane,
London SW18 4ES, England, a theatre that features European and Asian
classics and new works to a wide audience.

Bildquellen:
|National Theatre, London: Hugo Glendinning Titel. |Picture-Alliance GmbH,
Frankfurt/M.: dpa 4.1.

Wir arbeiten sehr sorgfältig daran, für alle verwendeten Abbildungen die
Rechteinhaberinnen und Rechteinhaber zu ermitteln. Sollte uns dies im Einzelfall
nicht vollständig gelungen sein, werden berechtigte Ansprüche selbstverständlich
im Rahmen der üblichen Vereinbarungen abgegolten.

Druck A⁴ / Jahr 2024
Alle Drucke der Serie A sind im Unterricht parallel verwendbar.

Redaktion: Angela Wesser, Stuttgart
Umschlagkonzeption: Blum Design und Kommunikation, Hamburg
Umschlagrealisation: Harald Thumser, Frankfurt
Druck und Bindung: Westermann Druck GmbH, Georg-Westermann-Allee 66,
38104 Braunschweig

ISBN 978-3-425-04858-1

Table of Contents

Biography of Hanif Kureishi

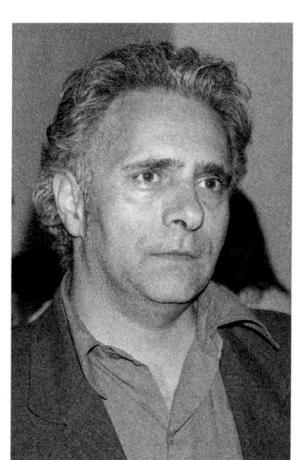

Playwright[1], screenwriter, novelist and film-maker Hanif Kureishi [kuˈreʃi] was born in Bromley, Kent in 1954 and read[2] philoso-
5 phy at King's College, London. His first play, *Soaking*[3] *the Heat*, was performed at the Royal Court Theatre in London in 1976 and was followed in 1980 by *The Mother Country*, for which he won the Thames TV
10 Playwright Award. In 1981 his play *Outskirts* won the George Devine Award and in 1982 he became Writer in Residence at the Royal Court Theatre.

His screenplay for the film *My Beautiful*
15 *Laundrette* was nominated for an Academy Award. The film was critically acclaimed[4] for its sensitive depiction[5] of a homosexual relationship between a gay skinhead and a young Asian man. He also wrote the screenplays for *Sammy and Rosie Get Laid*[6] and *London Kills Me* (1991), which he also directed. His film *My Son the*
20 *Fanatic* was adapted from his short story included in **Love in a Blue Time** (1997). This short story is also included in the Diesterweg anthology, **The Many Voices of English**. The film was first shown at the 1997 Cannes Film Festival. His play *Sleep With Me* (1999) was first performed at the National Theatre in London in 1999, and was followed by *When*
25 *the Night Begins* (2004), produced at the Hampstead Theatre in 2004.
Kureishi's first novel was the semi-autobiographical **The Buddha of Suburbia**, published in 1990. Karim, the novel's young hero, like Kureishi, has a Pakistani father and an English mother. The novel describes Karim's struggle for social and sexual identity, a comic coming-
30 of-age novel and a satirical portrait of race relations and the leftwing scene in Britain during the 1970s. It won the Whitbread First Novel

---

[1] playwright [ˈpleɪraɪt]: person who writes plays for the theatre, television or radio
[2] to read: (here): to study
[3] to soak: to take in
[4] to acclaim: to praise
[5] depiction: description, presentation
[6] to get laid (slang): to have sex

Award[7] and was produced by the BBC in 1993 as a four-part television series.

His second novel, **The Black Album** (1995), explores some of the issues facing the Muslim community living in Britain in the 1980s. **Love in a Blue Time,** his first collection of short stories, focuses on a series of 5 characters working in the media.

Intimacy (1998), a novella, is a painful account[8] of a man's decision to leave his partner and two young sons. It was produced as a controversial film in 2001; controversial because of its explicit sex scenes. His second short story collection, **Midnight All Day** (1999), continues to explore 10 very personal issues about human relationships and sexual desire.

Gabriel's Gift (2001) tells the story of a 15-year-old schoolboy whose artistic skills enable him to survive the trauma of his parents' separation. **Dreaming and Scheming: Reflections on Writing and Politics**, a collection of Hanif Kureishi's non-fiction, including essays and diary frag- 15 ments, as well as a new collection of short fiction, **The Body and Other Stories,** were both published in 2002. **The Word and the Bomb** (2005), is also a collection of non-fictional writings.

Hanif Kureishi's latest works are the play, *Venus* (2007), and the novel, **Something to Tell You** (2008). In 2009, his own stage adaptation of his 20 novel **The Black Album** (2009), premiered[9] at the National Theatre. He became a Commander of the Order of the British Empire[10] (CBE) in 2007, in recognition of his services to literature and drama.

His literary works centre on the social changes over recent decades, and the evolution of a multi-racial, multi-cultural Britain. While sympa- 25 thetic to the plight[11] of South-Asian immigrants, he stills cherishes[12] and upholds[13] the Western values of intellectual freedom that are threatened by religious intolerance and extremism (in this case extreme Islamism). For Kureishi Western values of intellectual freedom and extreme Islamism are the primary[14] combatants[15] in the Clash of Cultures. He has 30

---

[7] Whitbread First Novel Award: a major British literary award
[8] account: report, description
[9] to premier: to be performed for the first time
[10] Commander of the Order of the British Empire: an award given by the Monarch since 1917 to someone who has contributed significantly to the cultural life of Great Britain
[11] plight: difficult situation
[12] to cherish: to consider very dear and valuable
[13] to uphold: to support s.th. you consider right
[14] primary: main
[15] combatant: group or person involved in fighting a war

helped to bring the British-South-Asian experience into the mainstream and is now considered a major spokesman of this phenomenon.

The play, *The Black Album* by Hanif Kureishi was first performed at the National Theatre, London, on 14 July 2009. The year is 1989, to-
5 wards the end of the Thatcher[16] years when the *fatwa*[17] was imposed on[18] Sir Salman Rushdie[19] for his novel, **Satanic Verses**[20].

Bibliography

Borderline Methuen, 1981

Birds of Passage Amber Lane Press, 1983

Outskirts and Other Plays Calder, 1983

My Beautiful Laundrette Faber and Faber, 1986

Buddha of Suburbia Faber and Faber, 1990

London Kills Me: Screenplay Faber and Faber, 1991

The Black Album Faber and Faber, 1995

The Faber Book of Pop (editor with Jon Savage) Faber and Faber, 1996

Love in a Blue Time Faber and Faber, 1997

Intimacy Faber and Faber, 1998

My Son, the Fanatic (screenplay) Faber and Faber, 1998

Midnight All Day Faber and Faber, 1999

Sleep with Me Faber and Faber, 1999

Gabriel's Gift Faber and Faber, 2001

---

[16] Margaret Thatcher (1925–   ): Prime Minister of Great Britain 1979–1990 – She was known for her conservative economic policy and anti-union position.

[17] fatwa ['fætwɑː]: a religious decree *(Erlass)* by a Muslim leader – In this case it was a call for Sir Rushdie's execution by Ayatollah Khomeini, the former leader of Iran, in 1989.

[18] to impose on: to place on s.o.

[19] Sir Salman Rushdie (1947–   ): major British-Indian writer

[20] Satanic Verses: According to fanatic Muslims, the novel insulted Muslims and their religion. Sir Rushdie had to go into hiding for a number of years for fear of losing his life.

Dreaming and Scheming: Reflections on Writing and Politics Faber and Faber, 2002

The Body and Other Stories Faber and Faber, 2002

The Mother Faber and Faber, 2003

My Ear at His Heart Faber and Faber, 2004

When The Night Begins Faber and Faber, 2004

The Word and the Bomb Faber and Faber, 2005

Venus Faber and Faber, 2007

Something to Tell You Faber and Faber, 2008

The Black Album (play) Faber and Faber, 2009

Newness in the World

An Introduction to *The Black Album* – The Play
by Hanif Kureishi

It was in the summer of 2008 that I suggested to Jatinder Verma[1] that
5 we attempt a theatrical dramatisation of my second novel, **The Black
Album**.

The Black Album was a novel I had begun to think about in 1991, not
long after the publication of my first book, **The Buddha of Suburbia**.
Unlike that story, which I'd been trying to tell in numerous versions
10 since I first decided to become a writer, aged fourteen, **The Black Album**
was more or less contemporary, a "state of Britain" narrative not unlike
those I'd grown up watching, enthralled[2] and excited, in the theatre, particularly the Royal Court[3], and on television.

Around the time of its original publication in 1993, and after the BBC
15 film of **The Buddha of Suburbia**, there had been talk of filming **The
Black Album**. But instead of returning to something I'd just written
and was relieved[4] to have done with, it seemed easier to write a new
piece, with similar themes. This was *My Son the Fanatic,* a film set in
the North[5], and shot[6] in and around Halifax[7], starring Rachel Griffiths[8]
20 and Om Puri[9].

However, as the twentieth anniversary of the *fatwa*[10] was approach-
ing[11], and with **The Black Album** set in 1988–89 and concentrating on a

---

[1] Jatinder Verma (1954–): South-Asian born in Kenya – His family had to leave
Kenya in 1968 and settled in Great Britain. He is a theatre director and co-founder
of the theatre group Tara Arts with an emphasis on plays about the South-Asian
experience in Great Britain.
[2] to enthral: to captivate, to completely capture your interest
[3] the Royal Court: i.e., the Royal Court Theatre in London
[4] relieved: no longer feeling worry or anxiety
[5] the North: in northern England
[6] to shoot: (here) to film
[7] Halifax: city 60 km north-east of Manchester
[8] Rachel Griffiths (1968–): Australian actress
[9] Om Puri (1950–): Indian actor
[10] fatwa ['fætwɑː]: a religious decree *(Erlass)* by a Muslim leader – In this case it was a
call for Sir Salman Rushdie's execution by Ayatollah Khomeini, the former leader
of Iran, in 1989 because his novel, **Satanic Verses** was considered an insult to Muslims and their religion.
[11] to approach: to come near

small group of religious extremists, both Jatinder and I thought that my pre-7/7[12] novel might shed some light on[13] some of the things which had happened since.

Not that I had read the novel since writing it; and if I felt hesitant – as I did – to see it revived in another form, it was because I was anxious that in the present mood, after the bombings and atrocities[14], it might, in places, seem a little frivolous[15]. But the young radical Muslims I came to know at the time did appear to me to be both serious and intelligent, as well as naive, impressionable and half mad, and my account[16] of their activities and language reflected[17] what I learned in mosques[18] and colleges. The novel records[19] the kind of debates they had. And it wasn't as though the subject of liberalism[20] and its relation to extreme religion had gone away.

It was debate, ideological confrontation and physical passion that Jatinder and I had in mind when we sat down to work on the translation from prose to play. The novel, which has a thriller[21]-like structure, is a sprawl[22] of many scenes in numerous locations: foul[23] pubs, a further education college, a mosque, clubs, parties, a boarding house[24], cafés, Deedee[25]'s house and the street. As it was impossible in the theatre to retain[26] this particular sense of late-eighties London, we had to create longer scenes and concentrate on the important and even dangerous ar-

---

[12] 7/7: i.e., the 7 July 2005 London bombings – They were a series of coordinated suicide attacks upon Londoners using the public transport system during the morning rush hour. Four militants detonated four bombs, three on London Underground trains in quick succession. A fourth bomb exploded an hour later in a double-decker bus in Tavistock Square. Fifty-six people, including four bombers, were killed by the attacks with about 700 injured.

[13] to shed light on s.th.: to help to explain s.th.

[14] atrocity: a cruel and violent act

[15] frivolous ['frɪvələs]: silly, not serious or sensible

[16] account: report

[17] to reflect: to show, to express

[18] mosque [mɒsk]: *Moschee*

[19] to record: to make a written copy

[20] liberalism: Western values of democracy and sexuality

[21] thriller: a story about crime or spying

[22] sprawl [sprɔːl]: (here): a loosely connected group

[23] foul: dirty and smelling bad

[24] boarding house: a private house with rooms to rent and meals

[25] Deedee: a teacher at the further education college with whom the protagonist has an affair

[26] to retain: to keep

guments between the characters as they interrogated[27] Islam, liberalism, consumer[28] capitalism, as well as the place and meaning of literature and the way in which it might represent criticism of religion.

The first draft[29] was too much like a film and would have been un-
5 wieldy[30] to stage. Jatinder reminded me that we had to be ruthless[31]. He also reminded me, with his persistence[32] and imagination, how much I've learned about editing from the film and theatre directors I've worked with. If we were to create big parts for actors in scenes set in small rooms, we needed to turn prose into fervent[33] talk, having the conversation carry
10 the piece[34]. We had to ensure the actors had sufficient material to see their parts clearly. Each scene had to be shaped. The piece had to work for those who hadn't read the book.

It was this we worked on over a number of drafts, and it was the usual business of writing: cutting, condensing[35], expanding[36], developing, put-
15 ting in jokes and trying material in different places until the story moved forward naturally. I was particularly keen[37] to keep the humour and banter[38] of students and their often adolescent[39] attitudes, particularly towards sexuality. This was, after all, one of their most significant terrors: that the excitement the West offered would not only be too much
20 for them, but for everyone.

The *fatwa* against Salman Rushdie in February 1989 had reignited[40] my concern[41] about the rise of Islamic radicalism, something I had become aware of while in Pakistan in 1982, where I was writing **My Beautiful Laundrette**. But for me that wasn't the whole story. Much else of interest

---

[27] to interrogate: to ask a lot of questions about s.th.
[28] consumer: *Verbraucher*
[29] draft: rough written version of s.th. that is not yet in its final form
[30] unwieldy [ʌnˈwiːldi]: difficult to control or organise because of being too compli-
    cated
[31] ruthless: hardhearted, showing no mercy, cruel
[32] persistence: the act of continuing with s.th. in spite of resistance or opposition
[33] fervent: very passionate
[34] the piece: the play
[35] to condense: to reduce in size
[36] to expand: to increase in size
[37] keen: wanting to do s.th.
[38] banter: light, joking conversation
[39] adolescent: teenager
[40] to reignite: to cause to quickly begin again
[41] concern: *Sorge*

was happening around the end of the eighties: the music of Prince[42]; the collapse of Communism and the Velvet Revolution[43]; the rise of the new dance music[44] along with the use of a revelatory[45] new drug, Ecstasy[46]; Tiananmen Square[47]; Madonna[48] using Catholic imagery[49] in *Like a Prayer*[50], and post-modernism[51], "mash-ups[52]" and the celebration of hybridity[53] – of exchange and creative contamination[54] – which is partly the subject of **The Satanic Verses**.

This was also the period, or so I like to think, when Britain became aware that it was changing, or, in effect, had already changed from a monocultural to a multi-racial society, and had realised, at last, that 10

5

---

[42] Prince (1958–): Prince Rogers Nelson – U.S. rock singer, songwriter, record producer, and multi-instrumentalist. His albums include **Dirty Mind** (1981), **Purple Rain** (1984), **Parade** (1986), and **Emancipation** (1996). He changed his stage name to a symbol and is often referred to as "The Artist formerly known as Prince." Prince pioneered the "Minneapolis sound", a hybrid mixture of funk, rock, pop, R&B and New Wave that has influenced many other musicians. **The Black Album** is a Prince record that was originally planned for release on December 7, 1987, but at the last minute his record company decided not to offer it on the market. An enormous number of bootleg (illegal) copies changed hands.

[43] Velvet Revolution: the non-violent revolution in Czechoslovakia in 1989 that resulted in the overthrow of the communist government

[44] new dance music: e.g., House: a combination of disco, soul, R&B, funk, with messages about dancing, love, and sexuality

[45] revelatory (formal): making you aware of s.th. that was unknown before

[46] Ecstasy: a drug that causes a feeling of extreme happiness – It began to be abused by the youth culture in the 1970s.

[47] Tiananmen Square: square in the centre of Beijing, China that was the scene of a student protest in 1989, violently put down by the Chinese government

[48] Madonna (1958–): Madonna Louise Ciccone – American recording artist and actress

[49] imagery: words that create an image in the mind

[50] Like A Prayer: 1989 pop song that hints at sexual intercourse

[51] post-modernism: a term used to describe an attitude towards literature after World World II that doubts it is possible to create truly new and original literature in the future, and considers all literature in roughly the last 60 years as simply a reworking of all previous literature – Post-modern writers such as Paul Auster and Sir Salman Rushdie have indeed created a new kind of literature that playfully combines fragments of previous literature or literary genres in their works.

[52] mash-up: a song that places a previous vocal recording on another previous instrumental recording

[53] hybridity: a term used in the discussion of post-colonial literature that has various definitions according to the school of thought – In general it is used in the context of globalisation and migration to describe the mixing of Western culture, literature, and language with that of the former colonies and includes the debate whether such a mixture is possible or even desirable.

[54] contamination: the instance of making s.th. impure by mixing

there was no going back. This wasn't a mere confrontation with simple racism, the kind of thing I'd grown up with, which was usually referred to as "the colour problem." (When I was a young man it was taken for granted that to be Black or Asian was to be inferior to the white man.
5 And not for any particular reason. It was just the case: a fact.)

No, it was much more. Almost blindly, in the post-war period, a revolutionary, unprecedented[55] social experiment had been taking place in Britain. The project was to turn – out of the end of the Empire[56] and on the basis of mass immigration – a predominantly[57] white society into a
10 racially mixed one, thus forming a new notion of what Britain was and would become.

And now was the time for this to be evaluated. The *fatwa* in 1989, and the debate and arguments it stimulated, seemed to make this clear. Was it not significant that many of these discussions were about language?
15 The Iranian condemnation of a writer had, after all, been aimed at his words. What, then, was the relation between free speech and respect? What could and could not be said in a liberal society? How would different groups in this new society relate – or rather, speak – to[58] one another? How far could they go? What were the limits?
20 The coercive[59] force of language was something I had long been aware of. As a mixed-race child growing up in a white suburb, the debased[60] language used about immigrants and their families had helped fix and limit my identity. My early attempts to write now seem like an attempt to undo this stasis[61], to create a more fluid and complicated self through
25 storytelling. One of the uses of literature is that it will enable individuals to enlarge their sense of self – their vocabulary, the store[62] of ideas they use to think about themselves.

In the 1970s, many of us became aware, via[63] the scrutiny[64] of the gay, feminist and Black movements, of the power that language exerted[65]. If

---

[55] unprecedented: that has never happened before
[56] Empire: i.e. the British Empire
[57] predominantly: mainly
[58] to relate to s.o.: to interact with and be able to understand s.o.
[59] coercive: using force or the threat of force
[60] debased: made lower in quality or value
[61] stasis (formal): a situation in which there is no change or development
[62] store: a large supply to be used at a later time
[63] via: by means of
[64] scrutiny (formal): careful examination
[65] to exert: to use influence or authority to affect s.th. or s.o.

the country was to change – excluding fewer people – so did the discourse[66], and why not? Language, which implicitly[67] carried numerous meanings, developed all the time through creative use and misuse; if it was never still it could be revised[68], coaxed[69] in other directions. There were terms[70] applied to[71] certain groups which were reductive[72], stupid, humiliating[73], oppressive[74]. (Children, of course, are described constantly by their parents in ways which are both narrowing and liberating – and they have a good idea of what it is to live in an authoritarian world. It wasn't for nothing that I had been fascinated in my late teens by Wittgenstein[75]'s apothegm[76], "The meaning of a word is its use.")

If there was to be better speaking, the language had to be policed in some way, the bad words being replaced by the good. This, of course, became known as political correctness, where language was forced to follow a – usually leftist – political line. Inevitably[77], there was a backlash[78], as this form of political control seemed not only harsh[79] and censorious[80], but sometimes ludicrous[81] and irrelevant[82].

Liberals were in a tricky position, having to argue both for linguistic[83] protectionism[84] in some areas and for freedom in others. So that when some Muslims began to speak of "respect" for their religion and the

---

[66] discourse: the exchange of ideas
[67] implicitly: indirectly, in a way that suggests s.th.
[68] to revise: to change so as to make better
[69] to coax [kəʊks]: to seek to manipulate or persuade
[70] term: word, expression
[71] to apply to: to use s.th. for a certain purpose
[72] reductive: oversimplified, too generalised
[73] to humiliate: to make s.o. feel ashamed and stupid so as to cause a loss of self-respect
[74] oppressive: cruel, harsh, not fair
[75] Ludwig Josef Johann Wittgenstein (1889–1951): British philosopher, born in Austria – He explored the relationship of language to the world and argued that philosophical problems arise from insufficient attention to the variety of natural language use.
[76] apothegm ['æpəθem]: a short but not easily understood remark containing some general or generally accepted truth, maxim
[77] inevitably: unavoidably
[78] backlash: strong, negative reaction
[79] harsh: cruel, sever, unkind
[80] censorious: extremely critical, fault-finding
[81] ludicrous: absurd, ridiculous
[82] irrelevant: not important to or connected with a situation
[83] linguistic: connected with language or its scientific study
[84] linguistic protectionism: i.e., political correctness in the use of language

"insult" of **The Satanic Verses**, the idea of free speech and its neces-
sity and extension[85] was always presented as the conclusive[86] argument.
Criticism was essential in any society. This could be said, but not *that*.
But how would this be decided, and by whom?

5   The Marxists, too, were finding the issue of the *fatwa* difficult. It was
only partly a coincidence[87] that Islamic fundamentalism came to the
West in the year that that other great cause, Marxist-Communism, disappeared. The character of the stuttering[88] socialist teacher in **The Black
Album** – Deedee Osgood's husband Brownlow – was partly inspired
10 by some of the strange convolutions[89] of the disintegrating[90] Left at the
time.

At a conference in Amsterdam in 1989 I remember arguing with John
Berger[91], who was insisting that complaints about **The Satanic Verses**
were justified, as they came from the downtrodden[92] proletariat. Why, he
15 said, would he want to support a privileged middle-class artist who was
– supposedly – attacking the deepest beliefs of an otherwise exploited
and humiliated Muslim working class? This seemed to me to be an eccentric[93] and perverse point of view, particularly from a writer who valued freedom, and when it was obvious that the opportunity to dissent[94],
20 to be critical of leaders and authorities – and to be free of censorship[95]
– was necessary for anyone to live a good life, as the many writers, critics
and journalists in prison in Muslim countries would no doubt attest[96].

---

[85] extension: additional situations or contexts
[86] conclusive: putting an end to doubt, decisive, final
[87] coincidence: a chance occurrence of events remarkable for happening at the same
time or having some apparent connection
[88] to stutter: to have difficulty speaking because you cannot stop yourself from repeating the first sound of some words several times
[89] convulsion: (here): a sudden, often violent, political change that takes place in a
country
[90] to disintegrate: to fall apart
[91] John Berger (1926–   ): John Peter Berger – English art critic, novelist, painter,
and author
[92] downtrodden: oppressed
[93] eccentric [ɪkˈsentrɪk]: considered strange and unusual
[94] to dissent: to have or express opinions that are different from those that are officially accepted
[95] censorship: *Zensur*
[96] to attest: to affirm *(bestätigen)* that s.th. is true or correct

To struggle my way through this thicket[97] of fine distinctions[98], difficult debates and violent outcomes, I invented the story of Shahid[99], a somewhat lost and uncertain Asian kid from Kent[100], whose father has recently died – and who joins up, at college, with a band of similar-minded anti-racists. The story develops with Shahid discovering that the   5
group are going further than anti-racist activism. They are beginning to organise themselves not only around the attack on Rushdie, but as Islamo-fascists who believe themselves to be in possession of the Truth.

This is a big intellectual leap[101]. As puritanical[102] truth-possessors, Riaz's group and those they identify with have powerful, imperialistic 10
ideas of how the world should be and what it should be purged of[103]. Soon, believing the West has sunk into a stew[104] of decadence[105], consumerism[106] and celebrity obsession[107] – a not untypical fantasy about the West, corresponding to[108] a not unsimilar fantasy of the West about the sensual[109] East, as Edward Said[110] has argued – they believe it is their 15
duty to bring about a new, pure world. They want to awaken benighted[111] people to the reality of their situation. To do this they insist on a complete dominance of people's private lives, and of women and female sexuality in particular.

---

[97] thicket (fig.): *(Dickicht)*, (here): a large number of things that are not easy to understand or separate
[98] fine distinctions: differences that are so similar that they are not easy to determine or separate
[99] Shahid: in the novel and play he is of Pakistani extraction
[100] Kent: a county in south-east England
[101] intellectual leap (fig.): a conclusion that is not logical or easy to follow
[102] puritanical: having to do with Puritanism, characterised by moral and religious strictness and opposition to all pleasures as was typical of the Puritans in 17th century England and America
[103] to purge s.th. of s.th.: to rid s.th. of impure or undesirable elements
[104] stew [stju:] (fig.): unpleasant or undesirable state
[105] decadence: immoral behaviour or attitudes which show a fall in standards, and only an interest in pleasure and enjoyment
[106] consumerism: the belief that it is desirable for people to constantly buy things they really don't need to help the economy
[107] celebrity obesession: an unreasonable interest in the life of famous people
[108] corresponding to: equivalent to
[109] sensual: interested in physical pleasure and sex
[110] Edward Said [saːˈiːd] (1935–2003): Palestinian-American literary theorist — He was Professor of English and Comparative Literature at Columbia University and an important scholar specialising in post-colonialism. He is best known for his book **Orientalism** (1978), in which he criticised Western scholarship's attitude towards the Orient as being ethnocentric and arrogant.
[111] benighted: ignorant, existing in a state of intellectual darkness

Some of these attitudes were familiar to me, as I grew up in the sixties and seventies when the desire for revolution, for violent change, for the cleansing of exploitative[112] capitalists and a more ethical world, was part of our style. Almost everyone I knew had wanted, and worked in some
5 way to bring about, not only the modification[113] of capitalism, but its overthrow[114]. For us, from D. H. Lawrence[115] to William Burroughs[116] and the Sex Pistols[117], blasphemy[118] and dissent was a blessed[119] thing, kicking open the door to the future, bringing new knowledge, freedom and ways of living. The credo[120] was: be proud of your blasphemy,
10 these vile[121] idols have been worshipped[122] for too long! The point was to be disrespectful, to piss on the sacred[123] and attack authority. As Guy Debord[124] wrote, "Where there was fire, we carried petrol."

But there was, mixed in with this liberation rhetoric, as in other revolutionary movements – either of the left or right – a strong element of
15 puritanism and self-hatred. There was a desire for the masochism[125] of obedience[126] and self-punishment, something not only illustrated by the

---

[112] exploitive: taking advantage of s.o. in an unjust or unethical way

[113] modification: the act of making small changes, usually to improve s.th.

[114] overthrow: removal

[115] David Herbert Lawrence (1885–1930): British novelist, poet, and short-story writer. Many of his works deal with the destructiveness of modern industrial society, contrasted with the beauty of nature and instinct, especially the sexual impulse. His novels include **Sons and Lovers** (1913), **The Rainbow** (1915), **Women in Love** (1920), and **Lady Chatterley's Lover** (1928).

[116] William Seward Burroughs ['bʌrəʊz] (1914–1997): U.S. novelist, noted for his experimental works exploring themes of drug addiction, violence, and homosexuality. His novels include **Junkie** (1953), **The Naked Lunch** (1959), and **Interzone** (1989)

[117] Sex Pistols: controversial English punk rock band that formed in London in 1975 – They were responsible for initiating the punk movement in the United Kingdom, inspiring many later punk and alternative rock musicians.

[118] blasphemy: behaviour or using expressions that show a complete disrespect for a deity or religion

[119] blessed ['blesɪd]: (here): worthy of deep respect

[120] credo ['kreɪdəʊ]: formal statement of beliefs

[121] vile: terrible, evil, wicked

[122] to worship: to show great respect for a god or God, to adore

[123] sacred ['seɪkrɪd]: that which is considered to be holy

[124] Guy-Ernest Debord (1931–1994): French writer, filmmaker, artist, and revolutionary – He was a radical critic of capitalism and consumerism.

[125] masochism: the enjoyment of pain

[126] obedience [əˈbiːdɪəns]: the quality of always doing what you are told to do

Taliban[127], but by all revolts, which are inevitably vitiated[128] by the egotism of self-righteousness[129] and in love with self-sacrifice[130]. This concerns[131] not only the erotics of the "revolutionary moment", the ecstasy of a break with the past and the fantasy of renewal, but also the human penchant for[132] living in authoritarian societies and intransigent[133] systems, where safety and the firm[134] constraint[135] of the leader are preferable to liberal doubt, uncertainty and change. As George Bataille[136] reminds us in an essay written in 1957, "Man goes constantly in fear of himself. His erotic urges[137] terrify him."

Riaz, the solemn, earnest and clever leader of the small group which Shahid joins, understands that hatred of the Other[138] is an effective way of keeping his group not only together but moving forward. To do this, he has to create an effective paranoia[139]. He must ensure[140] that the image and idea of the Other is sufficiently horrible and dangerous to make it worth being afraid of. The former colonialistic Western Other, having helped rush the East into premature[141] modernity, must have no virtues[142]. Just as the West has generated[143] fantasies and misapprehensions[144] of the East for its own purposes, the East – this time stationed

---

[127] Taliban: a fundamentalist Islamic army in Afghanistan that seized control of the country in 1996 – Attempts to militarily remove the influence of the Taliban by Western forces since 2001 have not been successful.

[128] to vitiate ['vɪʃieɪt]: to make imperfect, to pervert, to corrupt

[129] self-righteousness: the quality of feeling or behaving as if what you say or do is always morally right, and other people are wrong

[130] self-sacrifice: *Selbstopferung*

[131] to concern: to have to do with s.th.

[132] penchant for: liking or fondness for s.th.

[133] intransigent: unwilling to change one's attitude or behaviour

[134] firm: strong and steady

[135] constraint: s.th. that limits or restricts, restriction

[136] George Bataille [ba'taj] (1897–1962): French writer and philosopher

[137] urge: strong desire

[138] the Other: a psychological term also used in a discussion of post-colonial literature to describe the fear and feeling of superiority that the West has felt towards people in its former colonies because of their being different, or it can be the reverse, whereby those in the former colonies still feel unfairly treated or oppressed by the former Western colonial powers

[139] paranoia [ˌpærə'nɔɪə]: an abnormal fear that other people are trying to harm you

[140] to ensure: to make sure

[141] premature: happening too soon

[142] virtue: *Tugend*

[143] to generate: to create

[144] misapprehension (formal): false idea

in the West – will do the same, ensuring not only a comprehensive[145] misunderstanding between the two sides, but a complete disjunction[146] which occludes[147] complexity.

Of course, for some Muslims this disjunction is there from the start.
5 To be bereft of[148] religion is to be bereft of human value. Almost unknowingly, Muslims who believe this are making a significant sacrifice by forfeiting[149] the importance of seeing others, and of course themselves, as being completely human. In Karachi[150], I recall, people were both curious and amazed when I said I was an atheist. "So when you
10 die," said one of my cousins, "you'll be all dressed up with nowhere to go?" At the same time Islamic societies, far from being "spiritual," are – because of years of deprivation[151] and envy[152] – among the most materialistic on earth. Shopping and the mosque have no trouble in getting along together.
15 Some of the attitudes among the kids I talked to for **The Black Album** reminded me of Nietzsche[153]'s analysis of the origins of religion, in particular his idea that religion – and Nietzsche was referring to Christianity – was the aggression of the weak, of the victim[154] or oppressed[155]. These attacks on the West, and the religion they were supposed to protect, were
20 in fact a form of highly organised resentment or bitterness, developed out of colonialism, racism and covetousness[156]. The violent criticism of Rushdie, an exceptionally gifted[157] artist of whom the community should have been proud, was in fact a hatred of talent and of the exceptional, a kind of forced equalisation[158] from a religion which had not only become

---

[145] comprehensive: of broad content
[146] disjunction: separation
[147] to occlude: to prevent, to block
[148] bereft of (formal): completely lacking s.th.
[149] to forfeit ['fɔːfɪt]: to lose, to allow to be taken away
[150] Karachi [kə'rɑːtʃi]: major port in south Pakistan
[151] deprivation: the state of lacking education, enough food, a decent place to live
[152] envy ['envi]: *Neid*
[153] Friedrich Wilhelm Nietzsche (1844–1900): German philosopher, poet, and critic, noted especially for his concept of the superman and his rejection of traditional Christian values. His most important works are **The Birth of Tragedy** (1872), **Thus Spake Zarathustra** (1883–1891), and **Beyond Good and Evil** (1886)
[154] victim: *Opfer*
[155] to oppress: *unterdrücken*
[156] covetousness ['kʌvɪtəsnəs]: jealousy because you want to have the possessions s.o. else has
[157] gifted: talented
[158] equalisation: the act of making everything equal and the same

culturally and intellectually mediocre[159], but which was looking to an invented past for solutions to contemporary[160] difficulties.

Towards the end of **The Black Album**, with the help of his lecturer[161] and soon-to-be-girlfriend Deedee Osgood, Shahid understands that he has to withdraw from[162] this group in order to establish himself on his own terms[163] at last. This isn't easy, as the group has provided[164] him with solidarity, friendship and direction, and doesn't want to let him go.

He extracts himself[165], in part, by beginning to discover the exuberance[166] and freedom of his own sexuality and creativity. "How does newness come into the world? How is it born? Of what fusions, translations, conjoinings[167] is it made?" asks Salman Rushdie, relevantly, at the beginning of **The Satanic Verses**.

It is also no accident that British and American pop, as exemplified[168] for Shahid by Prince's intelligent, sensual and prolific[169] creativity, is in a particularly lively phase. The clubs and parties Deedee takes Shahid to represent a continuing form of the youthful celebration and self-expression that Britain has enjoyed since the sixties.

If, along with mythology, religions are among man's most important and finest creation – with God perhaps being his greatest idea of all – Shahid also learns how corrupt and stultifying[170] these concepts can become if they fetishise[171] obedience and ritual, if they are not renewed and rethought. Like language itself, they can become decadent, and newness doesn't have an easy time. Blasphemy is as old as God and as necessary; religion and blasphemy are made for one another. Without blasphemy religion has no potency[172] or meaning. There's nothing like a

---

[159] mediocre [ˌmiːdiˈəʊkə]: average or ordinary in quality
[160] contemporary: belonging to the present time
[161] lecturer: a teacher at a university who is not a professor
[162] to withdraw from: to leave
[163] on your own terms: according to your own conditions
[164] to provide: to give, to grant
[165] to extract yourself: to separate yourself from s.th.
[166] exuberance: energy, happiness, excitement
[167] conjoining: the act of joining together
[168] to exemplify: to be a typical example
[169] prolific: producing many works
[170] stultifying (formal): making you feel very bored and unable to think of new ideas
[171] to fetishise: to deal with s.th. as an obsession (*fixe Idee*)
[172] potency ['pəʊtnsi]: power, strength

19

useful provocation to start a good conversation, and this can only be to the advantage of religion, keeping it tied to[173] scepticism[174].

In **The Black Album** it turns out that Shahid is one of the lucky ones, strong enough to find out – after flirting with extreme religion – that
5 he'd rather affect the world as an artist than as an activist. The others in his group are not so intelligent or objective; or perhaps they are just more passionate[175] for political change.

Whatever the reasons – and it is probably too late for psychological explanations – something had begun to stir[176] in the late eighties which
10 has had a profound[177] effect on our world, and which we are still trying to come to terms with[178].

---

[173] to tie to s.th.: *binden an*

[174] scepticism: an attitude of doubting that claims or statements are true or that s.th. will happen

[175] passionate: extremely eager

[176] to stir: (here): to begin to become active

[177] profound: very strong, very great

[178] to come to terms with: to accept s.th. new and sometimes unpleasant by learning to deal with it

The Black Album

by Hanif Kureishi

adapted for the stage from the novel by the author

The Black Album was first performed in the Cottesloe auditorium of the National Theatre, London, on 14 July 2009. The cast[1] was as follows:

Shahid Hasan Jonathan Bonnici	*Director* Jatinder Verma
Riaz al Hussain	*Set Designer* Tim Hatley
5 Alexander Andreou	*Costume Designer* Claudia Mayer
Strapper Glyn Pritchard	*Lighting Designer* Jvan Morandi
Hat Beruce Khan	*Video Designer* Tom Hadley
Deedee Osgood Tanya Franks	*Choreographer* Shobana Jeyasingh
Tahira/Zulma	*Music* Sister Bliss
10 Shereen Martineau	*Music Associate* John Gingell
Andrew Brownlow	*Sound Designer* Fergus O'Hare
Sean Gallagher	*Graphics and Animation*
Chad Nitin Kundra	Sara Nestruk
Chili Robert Mountford	

15

Characters

Shahid Hasan	*In a company of nine, other*
Strapper[2]	*characters may be doubled as*
Riaz al-Hussain	*follows*
Hat	Young Man, Councillor[7] Rudder,
20 **Chad**	Reporter (Strapper)
Deedee Osgood[3]	Heavy[8] 1 (Andrew Brownlow)
Andrew Brownlow[4]	Heavy 2 (Chad)
Chili[5]	Old Man, Cameraman (Chili)
Zulma[6]	Tahira, Mother (Zulma)

---

[1] cast: the actors, actresses in a play

[2] Strapper: In the novel Strapper is a young white man with blond hair, a drug dealer and drug addict.

[3] Deedee Osgood: In the novel she is described as a white woman in her thirties from a lower middle-class family.

[4] Andrew Brownlow: upper-class professor, Deedee Osgood's husband

[5] Chili: Shahid's brother

[6] Zulma: Chili's wife

[7] councillor: member of a council *(Gemeinderat)*

[8] heavy: actor who plays characters who are criminals, gangsters, or other unpleasant persons

Act One

SCENE ONE

Rural, suburban sounds, late afternoon. Lights fade up[9] on a map of the world, followed by the legend[10] HASAN TRAVELS. *Shahid enters, wrapped in an overcoat and carrying two suitcases. He puts them down and looks*   5
at the map and the legend. Mother enters.

Mother Arey[11], Shahid …!
She pulls a handkerchief out of his pocket, spits[12] on it and proceeds[13] to wipe his face.
     Going to college in London and so not smart.   10
Shahid (*protesting*) Ammi[14]…
Mother How happy your papa will be in paradise when you return with a college degree.
Shahid HND[15], Ammi …
Mother (*dismissive[16]*) Degree is a degree. (*Exclaims[17].*) My one son charms   15
     a beautiful girl like Zulma from Karachi[18] –
Shahid Not exactly difficult.
Mother Don't argue. Chili and Zulma are a golden couple. And you are about to charm books into a degree! Have you packed toothpaste? All-Bran[19]? Wake up, brush your teeth, have All-Bran with yoghurt   20
     and straightaway you will have perfect motions[20], smooth as the day is long. Promise me.
Shahid Yes, Ammi.

---

[9] to fade up: to increase the brightness of a dark area so that it can be increasingly better seen
[10] legend: a piece of writing
[11] arey (Urdu): *Meine Güte*!
[12] to spit, spat, spat: *spucken*
[13] to proceed: to do s.th. next
[14] Ammi (Urdu): mummy
[15] HND: Higher National Diploma, a higher education qualification in the United Kingdom equivalent to studying one or two years at a university, after which students can continue to study for a normal academic degree
[16] dismissive: showing that you don't believe s.th. is worth discussing
[17] to exclaim: to say suddenly and loudly with emotion
[18] Karachi [kə'rɑːtʃi]: chief port of Pakistan on the Arabian Ocean
[19] All-Bran®: breakfast cereal with high-fibre wheat – manufactured by the American firm Kellogg's that markets this cereal as an aid to digestion (*Verdauung*)
[20] motion (BE): *Stuhlgang*

Mother And ring. Every evening I want to hear progress report[21], just like your papa used to. Socks – have you packed enough?

Shahid Yes.

Mother Here's a kebab roll[22] to eat on the train –

5 **Shahid** I'm only going to London –

Mother You'll get hungry – why waste money? I've also precisely told Chili to take good care of you. He will visit often –

Shahid Oh, no.

Mother Listen to what he says. Packed the computer Papa bought you?

10 **Shahid** Of course.

Mother Papa will be so pleased. And Shahid?

Shahid What?

Mother Don't talk to strangers.

Shahid picks up his cases[23] and leaves. Mother hides her face in her sari[24]
15 *and starts crying. As he walks off, soundscape[25] gradually shifts to[26] polyglot[27] and frenetic[28] late-eighties London, and we see him journey to his north London digs[29]. Strapper bumps into[30] him.*

Strapper Want some E?

Shahid (*surprised*) What?

20 **Strapper** (*urgent[31]*) E, man – Ecstasy[32]! Want some?

Shahid No!

Strapper Keep your shirt on[33], Paki[34]!

Strapper runs off. Shahid arrives at his digs, unpacks his new Amstrad[35]
computer and sits down to work.

---

[21] progress report (incorrect English): a progress report
[22] kebab roll: a roll (*Brötchen*) with small pieces of meat cooked on a wooden or metal stick
[23] case: suitcase
[24] sari: traditional dress of women in India and Pakistan consisting of a narrow piece of cloth wrapped around the body
[25] soundscape: background noise
[26] to shift to: to change to
[27] polyglot: a mixture or confusion of many languages
[28] frenetic: nervous and energetic
[29] digs (BE): room or rooms you rent to live in
[30] to bump into: to hit a part of your body against s.o.
[31] urgent: *dringend*
[32] Ecstasy (slang): a powerful drug that acts as a stimulant and can produce hallucinations and extreme happiness
[33] Keep your shirt on!: Stay calm, don't get excited.
[34] Paki (slang): derogative (*abfällig*) way of addressing s.o. of Pakistani origin
[35] Amstrad: a British company that was a major producer of personal computers and word processors in the 1980s

As he works, London day and night life passes by in the rooms around him – lodgers[36] variously dancing, smoking dope, praying. Shahid is seen going between his computer and his bed, eating, reading, working and having a wank[37]. The light in his room flickers off[38].

Scene Two

Shahid's digs. There is a knock, followed by a door opening.

Riaz (*in Urdu*) *Khariat hait?* [All okay?]
Shahid (*startled, in Urdu*) *J-ji ... Aur aap?* [Yes ... And you?]
Riaz (*in Urdu*) *Jho Allah-tala ko manzoor ...* [Whatever Allah wills.]
   (*Introducing himself.*) Riaz Al-Hussain.   10
Shahid (*introducing himself*) Shahid Hasan.
Riaz You speak Urdu well.
Shahid Rusty[39].
The light flickers back on.
Riaz Have you eaten? When I am studying and writing I forget for hours 15
   to eat and then I remember that I am ravenous[40]. Are you like this?
Shahid Only when reading a good book.
Riaz You are searching for something.
Shahid Am I?
Riaz (*clears space[41] and settles himself in the room*) Come.   20
Shahid (*confused*) Where?
Riaz Sit, sit. I've ordered food from an excellent Pakistani takeaway[42]
   near here.
Shahid Thank you.
Riaz The boy will come soon. Where are you from?   25
Shahid Sevenoaks, Kent[43].
Riaz I am from Lahore[44] originally.

---

[36] lodger (BE): person who pays rent to live in a person's house
[37] wank (slang): the act of masturbation
[38] to flicker off: to shine with an unsteady light that becomes weaker until it is dark
[39] rusty (colloquial): not good because of a lack of practice
[40] ravenous: extremely hungry
[41] to clear space: to remove what is not wanted or needed in an area
[42] takeaway (BE): restaurant that sells meals that can be taken home
[43] Sevenoaks, Kent: commuter town 30 km south-east of London
[44] Lahore [lə'hɔ:]: capital of the Pakistan province of Punjab and the second largest city in Pakistan, after Karachi

Shahid That "originally" is a big thing.

Riaz You recognise that, eh[45]? You are a Pakistani at heart.

Shahid Well … not quite.

Riaz But yes. I have observed you before.

5 **Shahid** Have you? What was I doing?

Riaz You are hard-working. We all are who come here. I am without a doubt over your earnestness[46].

Shahid I'm desperate for good Indian food.

Riaz Naturally you miss such food.

10 *A knock on the door.*

Ah, here he is.

He opens the door to Hat, bringing the takeaway.

Meet Shahid – he's been living quietly in the room next to mine. A proper student!

15 **Hat** *Salaam-a-leikum[47].* I am Hat.

Shahid Shahid.

Riaz His father owns the takeaway. He is paying for him to study at the college.

Hat (*to Shahid*) Nice room, brother.

20 **Riaz** (*to Hat*) Have you brought your abha[48]'s famous brinjal pakoras[49] to start with?

Hat (*putting the takeaway cartons on Shahid's computer table*) Everything exactly as ordered. Kebab rolls as well.

Riaz (*exclaiming*) *Masha-Allah[50]!*

25 *He sits on the floor and opens the cartons.*

Come, Shahid – eat!

Hat (*to Riaz*) Papa very annoyed – he say definitely no more meetings in our café.

Riaz (*reassuring[51] as he eats*) We will respect his wishes. Don't worry

30 – now go.

Hat hesitates.

---

[45] eh: Don't you?

[46] earnestness: quality of being serious and sincere

[47] Salaam-a-leikum [sə'lɑːm ə 'leɪkʊm] (Arabic): Peace be upon you.

[48] abha (Urdu): father

[49] brinjal ['brɪnʒl] pakora [pə'kɔːrə]: deep-fried eggplant that has been covered with flour eaten as a snack in India and Pakistan

[50] Masha-Allah (Arabic): God has willed it! (expression of joy or praise)

[51] to reassure: to say s.th. that makes s.o. less frightened or worried

(*Realising.*) Ah! The money, of course. Take out a note from my pocket. Come, come, Shahid – this is the best food in London!

Hat fishes[52] *a fiver*[53] *out of Riaz's pocket, as Shahid joins him in eating.*

Shahid Are you a student too, Riaz?

Riaz Yes, of the law. Before, I gave only general and legal advice to the 5
many poor and uneducated people who came to see me in Leeds. But
now it is time to make a proper study. So, here I am in London – the
mecca[54] for all students, no[55]? (*Notices Hat standing by.*) You need
more money?

Hat (*brandishing*[56] *the fiver*) I have no change! 10

Riaz Arey[57], give it to me later. (*to Shahid*) Your family name is Hasan,
am I right?

Shahid Yes.

Riaz (*glowing*[58]) A family that bears[59] the name of the martyred[60] son of
Ali[61] can only be of great distinction[62]. 15

Hat browses[63] *through Shahid's bookshelf.*

Shahid I'd like to think so.

Riaz How, then, did they let you come to such a derelict[64] college?

Shahid Because I met a lecturer[65] called Deedee Osgood. I really liked
her. So I enrolled[66]. Do you know her? 20

Riaz Oh, yes, she has a reputation at the college.

Shahid At my interview, she only asked what I liked to read and the
music I listened to. I talked of **Midnight's Children**[67] – have you read
that?

---

[52] to fish: (here): to search and find s.th.
[53] fiver (BE, colloquial): five pound note
[54] mecca: holiest city of Islam in Saudi Arabia, (here): place that is often visited because of some attraction
[55] no (incorrect English): Isn't it?
[56] to brandish: to hold and wave about
[57] arey [əˈreɪ] (colloquial, Urdu): Oh, ho!
[58] to glow: to look very pleased and satisfied
[59] to bear (formal): to have
[60] martyred [ˈmɑːtəd]: *den Märtyrertod gestorben*
[61] son of Ali: Hasan ibn Ali, born in 625 A.D., related to Muhammad – An imam
(religious leader), he is said to have been poisoned.
[62] distinction: excellence of character
[63] to browse: to look through in a casual way
[64] derelict: falling into ruins, in a bad condition
[65] lecturer: a teacher at a university or college who is not a professor
[66] to enroll: to officially become a student, to register
[67] Midnight's Children: 1981 novel by Sir Salman Rushdie about the events surround-
ing India's independence from Great Britain

Riaz (*indicating*[68] *Hat browsing Shahid's shelf*) Hat has never seen a book before – he is an accountant[69]. (*Returning to Shahid's question.*) That book was accurate about Bombay. But this time he has gone too far.

5 **Shahid** When that writer got on TV and attacked racism, Riaz, I wanted to cheer. He spoke from the heart.

Riaz My abha spoke from the heart. He set me on the path of showing our suffering people their rights.

Shahid That's exactly what the man argued on TV – our rights against
10 racism.

Riaz How do you like the pakoras?

Shahid They taste just like my ammi's.

Hat Wicked[70], yaar[71]! I'll tell my abha. He be[72] dead[73] pleased.

Riaz (*to Shahid*) What does your abha do?

15 **Shahid** Travel agent. He bought the agency where he worked as a clerk when he first came to Sevenoaks.

Riaz (*exclaiming, with satisfaction at having polished off*[74] *a kebab roll*) Al-hum du'lilla[75] – he found his right path.

Shahid Mum runs the agency now with my brother Chili. His wife
20 Zulma's from Karachi.

Riaz While your papa enjoys a well-earned retirement[76]!

Shahid (*matter of fact*[77]) He died six months ago.

Riaz (*sympathetic, as he wipes his fingers on a handkerchief*) To pass your last days so far from home must have been very painful for
25 him.

Shahid Not Papa. Every evening he'd lie in bed in his smoking jacket[78] and entertain visitors like some pasha[79]. His "centre of operations",

---

[68] to indicate: to make s.o. notice s.th. by pointing or moving your head
[69] accountant: *Buchhalter, -in*
[70] wicked ['wɪkɪd] (slang): very good
[71] yaar (Indian, Pakistani English): my friend
[72] be: will be
[73] dead (colloquial): very
[74] to polish ['pɒlɪʃ] off (colloquial): to finish eating s.th.
[75] Al-hum du'lilla (Arabic): Praise to God! Thank God!
[76] retirement: *Ruhestand*
[77] matter of fact: said without showing any emotion when it would be expected
[78] smoking jacket: comfortable jacket made of velvet (*Samt*)
[79] pasha (humorous): like an important official of the Ottoman Empire

he'd call it, swigging[80] whisky and soda in a long glass, with Glenn
Miller[81] on the turntable[82].

Riaz looks at him.

Him[83] and Ammi – they'd never go anywhere themselves, apart from
Karachi once a year.   5

Riaz Your brother, he is in charge of the business now?

Shahid Chili? He has a looser attitude to work.

Riaz Is he a dissipater[84]?

Shahid bristles[85].

(*urging him on[86]*) Eat, eat!   10

Shahid complies[87].

What do our people really have in their lives?

Shahid Some have security and purpose at least.

Riaz They have lost themselves.

Shahid They've certainly lost something. My parents always despised[88]   15
their work and laughed at customers for boiling their bodies on foreign beaches.

Riaz Precisely right! No Pakistani would dream of being such an idiot
by the seaside – as yet. But soon – don't you think? – we will be parad-
ing about everywhere in these bikinis.   20

Shahid That's what my mother and Chili are waiting for. I've got to tell
you, Riaz – after Papa died – this is the truth now –

Riaz Anything less is worthless.

Shahid I lost it for a while[89]. Did badly at school. I'd, uh[90], got my girlfriend pregnant, and she'd had to have a late abortion[91]. I started   25

---

[80] to swig: to take a quick drink of s.th.
[81] Glen Miller (1904–1944): American composer, trombonist, and band leader. During World War II he was the leader of the U.S. Air Corps band in Europe. He
disappeared on a flight between England and France.
[82] turntable: the round surface on a record player on which you place the record to
be played
[83] him (incorrect English): he
[84] dissipater: person only interested in pleasure
[85] to bristle ['brɪsl]: to suddenly become annoyed at what s.o. says
[86] to urge s.o. on: to encourage s.o. to do s.th.
[87] to comply [kəm'plaɪ]: to obey an order
[88] to despise: to dislike very much
[89] I lost it for while.: I lived my life aimlessly.
[90] uh: sound made when a person is not sure what to say
[91] abortion: *Abtreibung*

hitting the clubs[92] after that, just bumming around[93]. I couldn't concentrate on anything. I wanted – wanted to – uh –

Riaz Yes, yes?

Chad enters.

5 **Chad** Riaz, brother –

Riaz gestures[94] for Chad to keep quiet.

Riaz (*to Shahid*) Speak openly – he is one of us.

Shahid I wanted to be a racist.

Chad What kind of thing are we talking about here?

10 **Shahid** Go around abusing[95] Pakis, niggers[96], Chinks[97], Irish, any foreign scum[98]. Slag[99] them under my breath[100]. Kick them up the arse[101].

Riaz Open your heart.

Shahid The thought of sleeping with Asian girls made me sick. I wouldn't touch brown flesh, except with a branding iron[102]. Even when they

15 came on to me[103], I couldn't bear it. I thought, you know, wink[104] at an Asian girl and she'll want to marry you up[105].

Riaz Oh, how is this done?

Chad You didn't want to be a racist. I'm telling you that here and now for definite. And I'm informing you that it's all all right now.

20 **Shahid** I am a racist.

Chad You only a vessel[106].

---

92 to hit the clubs (colloquial): to go to various clubs (a place where young people go to dance or listen to music)
93 to bum around (colloquial): to spend your time without a purpose or goal
94 to gesture: to move your hand or head for the purpose of communicating s.th.
95 to abuse: to treat a person or an animal in a cruel or violent way or to insult
96 nigger (slang): offensive word for a Black person
97 Chink (slang): offensive word for a Chinese person
98 scum (informal): worthless person
99 to slag (slang, BE): to criticise sharply
100 under your breath: quietly, in a whisper
101 arse (slang, BE): part of the body you sit on
102 branding iron: *Brandeisen*
103 to come on to s.o.: to make yourself sexually attractive to s.o.
104 to wink: *zwinkern*
105 to marry s.o. up (colloquial): to marry s.o.
106 vessel: (here): instrument for some purpose

Shahid I wanted to join the British National Party[107]. I would have filled in the forms if they have forms. How do you apply to such an organisation?

Chad Would the brother know? Listen. It been the longest, hardest century of racism in the history of everything. How can you not have picked up the vibe[108] in this distorted[109] way? There's a bit of Hitler in all white people – they've given that to you.

Riaz Only those who purify themselves can escape it. Racism turns us away from ourselves. But there is another way. I am honoured to know you, Shahid.

He hugs[110] him.

Shahid I'm pleased to have met you tonight.

Riaz Thank you. I too have learned.

Chad (*to Shahid*) I am hearing every moment of your soul cry. Call me Chad.

They embrace[111].

(*To Riaz.*) We need to sort[112] things for the meeting.

Riaz Hat's papa doesn't want us to meet in his café any more.

Chad But Tahira's bringing all the petitioners[113] there!

Riaz Tell her to delay[114] until we find another place – I have too many petitions[115] and letters to work on for everyone to meet in my room.

Shahid You can meet here.

Riaz (*delighted*) Al-hum du'lilla – you *are* a Pakistani at heart!

Shahid I'll just put my books and Prince collection away and –

---

[107] British National Party: far-right political party founded in 1982 that wants to make Britain all white and remove all non-white immigrants and their descendants

[108] to pick up the vibe (colloquial): to be affected and influenced by the political atmosphere

[109] distorted: *verzerrt*

[110] to hug: to put your arms around s.o. as a sign of affection

[111] to embrace: to hug

[112] to sort (colloquial, BE): to deal with a problem, to organise s.th. properly

[113] petitioner: a person along with others who signs a document requesting some form of action by a government or other authority

[114] to delay: to put off to a later time, to wait before taking action

[115] petition: written document requesting that some kind of action be taken by a government or authority

Information Box

Prince (1958–): Prince Rogers Nelson – U.S. rock singer, song-writer, record producer, and multi-instrumentalist. His albums include **Dirty Mind** (1981), **Purple Rain** (1984), **Parade** (1986), and
5 **Emancipation** (1996). He changed his stage name to a symbol and is often referred to as "The Artist formerly known as Prince." Prince pioneered the "Minneapolis sound," a hybrid mixture of funk, rock, pop, R&B and New Wave that has influenced many other musicians. He occasionally sang with a female voice and wore high-heeled shoes on
10 the stage. **The Black Album** is a Prince record that was originally planned for release on December 7, 1987, but at the last minute his record company decided not to offer it on the market. An enormous number of bootleg (made and sold illegally) copies changed hands. Prince did not concern himself with the Civil Rights Movement. By
15 the 1970s the Civil Rights Movement had achieved many of its goals anyway. His songs are often explicitly about sex. Hybridity is the keyword when describing Prince: in terms of his race (light-skinned African American), his appearing on the stage with both female and male characteristics, and his mixture of pop styles.

20 **Chad** (*quickly*) You say Prince?

Shahid Yeh[116], I've got all his records – even the *Black Album*.

Chad No way[117], man – I mean brother – that bootleg.

Shahid Picked it up in Camden Market[118].

Chad Right. Right. It good for bootlegs.

25 **Shahid** Want it?

Chad Never! We are slaves to Allah! He the only one we must submit to[119].

Shahid It's only music.

Riaz Only those who purify themselves can escape it.

30 **Chad** (*to Shahid*) The brother mean your soul – you got to clean yourself inside from all that white shit.

Shahid Prince is black.

---

[116] yeh (colloquial): yes

[117] no way (colloquial): There's no way I can accept that.

[118] Camden Market: market consisting of a series of stalls in Camden Town (a district in north-west London) that sell clothing, small decorative articles of little value, etc.

[119] to submit to: to accept the authority or control of s.o. or s.th.

Chad There's more to life than entertaining ourselves! Brother, you got a lot to learn.

Riaz gets up.

The brother need fresh air. We all do. Phew[120].

Riaz We are pleased to have you with us. 5

They leave.

Shahid returns to his computer. Music. The college bell rings.

Scene Three

Morning. A run-down[121], inner-city further education college. Noisy class. Wolf whistles[122] and comments fly as Deedee strides[123] through the room.

10

Deedee Our subject today is the Black struggle in America –

Various excited comments fly around the class.

– as reflected in popular culture.

She clicks on a slide: a photo of young Emmett Till[124]. Comments fly around on the look of this young, fresh-faced Black young man.

Fifteen-year-old Emmett Till – a boy living in Chicago in the 1950s. 15 One day, he went to visit his relatives who lived in a small town in Mississippi. On the High Street[125], he saw a young white woman –

Someone in class lets out a wolf whistle.

Stop that! He did it for a dare[126]. That night, the woman's husband and brother paid him a visit. They took him to a warehouse[127], broke his 20 wrists[128] and ankles[129], gouged out[130] his left eye and shot him through the head. Then, they tied his neck to a seventy-pound fan[131] used for

---

[120] phew [fjuː]: a sound made to express the experience of smelling s.th. unpleasant
[121] run-down: in bad condition because of not being cared for
[122] wolf whistle: a whistle a man makes when he sees an attractive woman passing by
[123] to stride: to walk with long steps
[124] Emmett Louis Till (1941–1955): Black American who was brutally murdered in Mississippi at the age of 14 after supposedly flirting with a white woman. In the trial that followed the murderers were found not guilty. The massive protest that followed gave the Civil Rights Movement an impetus.
[125] on the high street (BE): on main street (AE)
[126] for a dare: as a challenge to prove your courage
[127] warehouse: *Lagerhalle*
[128] wrist: *Handgelenk*
[129] ankle: *Fußgelenk*
[130] to gouge out: to remove by digging into the surface
[131] fan: *Ventilator*

winnowing cotton[132] and dumped[133] the body in a nearby river – where it was found by fishermen three days later. This is what Emmett Till looked like after his trip to the South.

She clicks on another slide – photo of Emmett Till in his coffin[134].

5   Emmett Till's mother wanted the whole world to see what had been done to her baby. So she insisted on an open coffin at his funeral.

Tahira How did the whites react?

Deedee Many accused her of being eager for[135] publicity –

Tahira That's blaspheming[136], right?

10 **Deedee** Only in the sense that it blasphemed the reality of what happened to her son.

Tahira So the blasphemers were racists?

Deedee You could say that.

She starts another set of slides, depicting[137] the Civil Rights Movement
15 *and popular Black musicians, writers, sportsmen and other artists.*

I want you to focus on the extraordinary creativity that emerged from[138] America by artists questioning segregation.

Shahid How's the music of Prince relate to[139] the Black struggles, miss?

Tahira Prince? He's a total dushman[140]!

20 **Hat** Yeah – he ain't apna[141].

Deedee Good question, Shahid. We'll make that the assignment[142] for next week – how Black musicians responded to racism.

Tahira Why you shoving[143] us always to music and them[144] fripperies[145] – what about the Nation of Islam[146]?

---

[132] to winnow cotton: to remove the seeds from the cotton plant
[133] to dump: to let fall heavily
[134] coffin: *Sarg*
[135] eager for: wanting very much, keen on
[136] to blaspheme [ˌblæsˈfiːm]: to show no respect for God or sacred things in word or deed
[137] to depict: to show in pictures
[138] to emerge from: to begin to appear
[139] to relate to: to be connected to s.o.
[140] dushman (Urdu): enemy
[141] apna (Urdu): one of us
[142] assignment: written task, homework
[143] to shove: to push in a rough way
[144] them (incorrect English): those
[145] frippery (BE): objects, decorations, etc. considered unnecessary and expensive
[146] Nation of Islam: Muslim African-American religious movement founded by Wallace D. Fard Muhammad in 1930 to improve the situation of Blacks in America. From 1934–1975, it was led by Elijah Muhammad, who established businesses and schools. Malcolm X (original name Malcolm Little) (1925–1965) was one of its leaders.

Deedee Let's have an essay from you on Malcolm X and how the Nation of Islam helped in the Black struggles, Tahira – when you can get your head out of Khalil Gibran[147]. The rest, concentrate on Black musicians. On my desk by next week. And as the mathematicians say, go forth[148] and multiply[149].   5

Hat (*emulating*[150] *a move*[151] *of Michael Jackson's*[152]) Thriller[153]! I'm bad[154]! *Tahira whacks*[155] *him. Laughter from the class as they disperse*[156] *while Deedee picks out Shahid.*

Deedee Why do you like Prince?

Shahid Well, the sound.   10

Deedee Anything else?

Shahid He's black.

Deedee And half white, half man, half woman –

Shahid Half size –

Deedee Feminist –   15

Shahid But macho[157] too.

Deedee He can play soul[158] and funk[159] –

Shahid And rock[160] and rap[161].

---

[147] Khalil Gibran (1883–1931): Lebanese-American artist, poet, and writer – He is chiefly known in the English speaking world for his 1923 book, **The Prophet**, a book consisting of twenty-six poetic essays. It became especially popular during the 1960s with the American counterculture and New Age movements.

[148] to go forth: to go away

[149] Go forth and multiply.: Cf. Genesis 1: 22, 28 "Be fruitful and multiply." and Genesis 9:1: "Be fruitful, and multiply, and replenish the earth." "Multiply" is used here as a mathematical operation and in the sense of having children. "Go forth and multiply" is also a slang expression for "Fuck off." (*Verpiss dich!*)

[150] to emulate: to imitate

[151] move: dance step

[152] Michael Joseph Jackson (1958–2009): extremely successful American recording artist, dancer, and singer-songwriter – He undertook a number of facial operations to remove his African characteristics.

[153] Thriller: album released by Michael Jackson in 1982

[154] I'm bad.: Bad was an album released by Michael Jackson in 1987.

[155] to whack: to hit very hard

[156] to disperse: to go away in many different directions

[157] macho ['mætʃəʊ]: showing pride in being masculine

[158] soul: a type of Black music resulting from the addition of jazz, gospel, and pop elements to the urban blues style

[159] funk: a type of polyrhythmic Black dance music with heavy syncopation

[160] rock: any of various styles of pop music having a heavy beat, having its origin in rock and roll

[161] rap: a style of pop music with a fast, rhythmic monologue over pre-recorded music

Deedee How are you coping[162]?

Shahid Never been so alone before. But I've run into people who excite me. Your lectures[163] fire me up to spend the time reading and writing.

5 **Deedee** You're a good student.

Shahid (*diffident*[164]) Could you – have a look at something I've written? About a friend?

Deedee (*offhand*[165]) How sad! (*Beat*[166].) Some of my other students are coming by later to eat and talk – why don't you join us? You can pore

10 through[167] my Prince videos.

Shahid I'd like that. Thank you.

Deedee pulls from her bag a copy of Salman Rushdie's **The Satanic Verses**[168] *and hands it to Shahid.*

Deedee Have you read this?

15 **Shahid** (*taking it*) Oh wow! Just the writer I've been talking about with my friends! Thanks.

He heads off to the canteen with the book. She lingers[169], *watching him as he joins Riaz, who is in discussion with Brownlow, flanked*[170] *by Chad, Hat and Tahira.*

20 **Riaz** Communism has been a good idea to bring into the world, Dr Brownlow. But its repressive[171] championing[172] of atheism goes against fundamental human impulses, don't you think?

Chad Right. Atheism only a tiny minority thing. Like transvestism[173].

Brownlow Y-y-you are confusing the p-p-practice with the ideal. That's like equating the Ch-Ch-Church with the Bible.

---

[162] to cope: to deal successfully with a situation, to manage

[163] lecture: *Vortrag*

[164] diffident: lacking self-confidence, shy

[165] offhand: not showing much interest

[166] beat: (here): A term used in stage directions to indicate a pause in the dialogue for the purpose of showing a significant shift in the direction of a scene. It is up to the actor or the director to decide what action should take place on the stage during this pause.

[167] to pore through (colloquial): to look at

[168] The Satanic Verses: novel published by Sir Salman Rushie in 1988 that caused a controversy in the Muslim world: Muslims accused him of blasphemy and mocking their faith. A *fatwa* (Erlass) was issued against him by Ayatollah Khomeini, the Supreme Leader of Iran, on February 14, 1989. It demanded his death.

[169] to linger: to stay longer than planned

[170] flanked: positioned on both sides

[171] repressive: limiting, controlling, oppressive

[172] to champion: to fight for in order to support a belief

[173] transvestism: the act of a man liking to dress as a woman

Riaz The idea can only be as good as the practice. You have to admit Communism everywhere has failed to wipe out[174] the base[175] human disease of racism. Without God people think they can sin[176] with impunity[177]. There is no morality.

Chad Only extremity[178], ingratitude[179], hard-heartedness, like Thatcher- 5 ism[180].

Riaz Capitalism in a nutshell[181], will you agree, Dr Brownlow?

Brownlow Oh, wh-wh-wholeheartedly[182]! Her destruction of the working classes is one of the crimes of the century.

Chad They been saying God dead. But it being[183] the other way round. 10 Without the creator no one knows where they are or what they doing.

Riaz *Allah-u-Akbar*[184]!

Deedee leaves.

All (*except Shahid*) *Allah-u-Akbar*! 15

Riaz We should pray.

Shahid Here?

Chad Allah's command overtop[185] all others, brother.

Riaz Will you join us, Dr Brownlow?

Brownlow (to *Riaz*) It w-w-would be an honour. I have papers to mark. 20 This e-e-evening? If you w-w-would lead me?

Riaz Of course, of course.

Brownlow leaves.

Shahid Who is Dr Brownlow?

Hat Teaches history here. A couple of decades back he was at the[186] 25 Cambridge University –

Chad The top student of his year.

---

[174] to wipe out: to get completely rid of

[175] base: of low moral quality

[176] to sin: *sündigen*

[177] with impunity: without being punished

[178] extremity [ɪkˈstreməti]: an extreme condition

[179] ingratitude: state of not feeling or showing that you are grateful for s.th.

[180] Thatcherism: the policy of Conservative Prime Minster (1979–1990), Margaret Thatcher (1925–   ), who was very business-friendly, reduced social services and benefits, and limited the influence of the unions

[181] in a nutshell (idiom): essentially, in essence *(auf den Punkt gebracht)*

[182] wholeheartedly: completely

[183] being (incorrect English): is

[184] Allah-u-Akbar (Arabic): God is the greatest!

[185] to overtop: to surpass, to be better than anything else

[186] the (incorrect English): Normally, a definite article would not be used here.

Hat Yeah, I'm telling you. He come from the upper middle classes. He could have done any fine thing. They wanted him at Harvard[187]. Or was it Yale[188], Chad?

Chad He refused them places down[189].

5 **Hat** Yeah, he told them to get lost[190]. He hated them all, his own class, his parents – everything. He come to this college to help us, the underprivileged niggers and wogs[191] and margin people[192]. He's not a bad guy – for[193] a Marxist-Communist –

Chad Leninist[194] –

10 **Tahira** Trotskyist[195] –

Hat Yeah, a Marxist-Communist-Leninist-Trotskyist type. He always strong on anti-racism. Isn't that right, brother Riaz?

Riaz Dr Brownlow has a good heart.

Chad Problem is –

15 **Hat** (*to Shahid*) Yeah, listen – problem is – he been developing this st-st-st-stutter.

Shahid It's a new thing then, is it?

Hat Yeah, it come on[196] since the Communist states of Eastern Europe began collapsing[197]. As each one goes over[198] he get another syllable on

20 his impediment[199], you know. In a lecture, it took him twenty minutes to get the first word out. He was going h-h-h-he-he … we didn't know if he was trying to say Helsinki, hear this, help, or what.

Shahid What was it?

Hat Hello.

---

187 Harvard: in Cambridge, Massachusetts: the oldest and most prestigious university in the USA

188 Yale: another prestigious university in New Haven, Connecticut, USA, founded in 1701

189 He refused them places down: correct English: He turned those places down.

190 Get lost! (colloquial): No way! (*Vergiss es!*)

191 wog [wɒg] (slang, racist): a non-white person

192 margin people: minority people who live at the edge of society

193 for: even if he is …

194 Leninist: a person who is a follower of Lenin (1870–1924), Marxist theoretician and first Premier of the Soviet Union

195 Trotskyist: a person who is a follower of Leon Trotsky (1879–1940) – He was opposed to Stalin's dictatorship.

196 come on: correct English: started

197 Communist … collapsing.: a reference to the end of Soviet influence in Eastern Europe in the late 1980s and the end of the Cold War

198 goes over (colloquial): collapses

199 he get … impediment (*Sprachstörung*): His stuttering gets worse with yet another syllable.

Chad By the time Cuba goes[200] he won't even manage that, I reckon[201].

Tahira You met his wife – Deedee Osgood.

Shahid She's his wife?

Chad She his wife.

Tahira Keep away from her.   5

Shahid Why?

Tahira Riaz has evidence that her family are nudists.

Beat, as the others consider the comment.

And she always watching *Top of the Pops*[202].

Shahid Really?   10

Chad Without God-consciousness[203] you can get away with everything. And when that happens you're lost. Now I know God is watching me. With him seeing every single damn thing, I have to be pretty careful about what I'm up to[204].

Shahid Like living in a greenhouse[205]?   15

Riaz Everything you do and think is witnessed[206]. Time to pray.

As Riaz and the others get ready to pray, a student walks through the group.

Chad Oi[207] – this here our multicultural democratic right, so fuck off[208]!

The student hurries off. Bell rings. Music, as they all disperse. Shahid re-   20
turns to his digs, putting away his copy of **The Satanic Verses**.

Scene Four

Shahid's digs. Evening. Shahid is dressing to go out. A knock on the door.

Shahid Come.

Chad enters.   25

Chad Hey, going somewhere, yaar?

---

[200] goes: (here): gets rid of its Communist regime

[201] to reckon (colloquial, BE): to think, to believe

[202] Top of the Pops: BBC television programme (1964–2006) in which the week's best-selling pop artists performed

[203] God-consciousness: acknowledging God, being aware of the presence of God

[204] to be up to s.th.: to be engaged in some activity, to be doing s.th.

[205] greenhouse: *Treibhaus*

[206] to witness: to observe closely

[207] Oi (colloquial, BE): exclamation used to attract s.o.'s attention, especially in an angry way

[208] Fuck off! (slang): Get lost! (*Verpiss dich!*)

Shahid Na, just a function[209], you know, student thing.

Chad Good, good. We need the room – expecting many more people coming to our meeting tonight.

Hat barges in[210].

5 **Hat** Hey, Shahid, there's someone looking for you.

Shahid Who?

Hat He wearing crocodile shoes.

Shahid (*quickly*) Please, Hat, say I had to go out.

Chad Hat don't tell no lies.

10 **Shahid** Sorry?

Hat No, I'm training to be an accountant.

Enter Chili, smartly dressed.

Chili How you doing, baby brother? Hug me, babe. Toot sweet[211].

They hug.

15 **Shahid** Chad, Hat, this is my brother Chili.

Hat Hi.

They shake hands.

Chili shakes hands with Chad, who then sniffs[212] his fingers and makes a face at Hat, as they leave.

20 **Chili** Where the hell to sit?

Shahid gathers[213] the manuscript to take to Deedee's.

Why are you being in a hurry with me, brother?

Shahid I'm not.

Chili You tapping[214] your foot.

25 **Shahid** I got an appointment[215], Chili.

Chili Pussy[216]?

Shahid No! A tutor[217] from the college.

Chili Ah-ha. You're starting to pull[218] – the family is delighted. Remember what Uncle Asif always said: "Your country's gone to the wogs, boys! Pakistanis in England now have to do everything – win the sports,

---

209 function: social event
210 to barge[bɑːdʒ] in: to enter a place interrupting what s.o. else is doing or saying
211 toot sweet: tout de suite (French): immediately
212 to sniff: to smell
213 to gather: to bring things together that have been spread out
214 to tap: to hit gently against s.th.
215 appointment: *Termin*
216 pussy (slang): (here): an opportunity for sex
217 tutor (BE): teacher, especially of adults
218 to pull (colloquial): to become active

present the news, run the shops and businesses, as well as fuck the
women. You've got the brown man's burden[219]."

Shahid Which you take on personally.

Chili Cool trousers. Tartan[220] suits you. They're not mine, are they?

Shahid No.   5

Chili Where's my red shirt?

Shahid What?

Chili Papa would be pleased. He always admired your brains. Got some
jimmi hat[221]?

Shahid is mystified[222].   10

    (*Explaining.*) Rubbers[223]. Johnnies[224]. You don't want no baby's mama
just yet, bro[225]. Not still doing that scribbling[226], are you?

Shahid What do you mean?

Chili I'll give you a slap[227] if you waste your time like that. How the hell
will you ever look relatives in the face?   15

He feints[228] a slap at Shahid, but turns it into a caress[229].

    That big boy, is he a new friend of yours?

Shahid Chad? Yes.

Chili Tell him if he sniffs his fingers at me again his children's children
will feel the pain.   20

Shahid Okay. What do you want, Chili?

Chili What is the world coming to, when a man can't visit his baby
brother?

Shahid You haven't shown much concern before.

Chili You know what Papa said to me before he died? "Take care of the   25
boy, don't let him go down, Chili."

---

[219] the brown man's burden: Cf. *The White Man's Burden*, a poem by the English
    writer, Rudyard Kipling (1865–1936) – In the poem he saw the necessity of the
    white man to civilise the natives of the colonies in the British Empire.
[220] tartan: a pattern of squares and lines of different colours and widths that cross
    each other, especially on cloth from Scotland
[221] jimmi hat (slang): condom
[222] mystified: confused, puzzled
[223] rubber (colloquial): condom
[224] johnny (slang): condom
[225] bro (colloquial): brother
[226] to scribble: (normally): to write s.th. quickly and carelessly because you are in a
    rush, (here): to write essays or works of literature
[227] slap: the acting of hitting with the flat part of the hand
[228] to feint [feɪnt] to confuse s.o. by making a movement that is expected but then not
    carried out
[229] caress: a gentle touch

Shahid He called me a bloody eunuch[230] fool for reading Shelley[231] to Sarah on my first date!

Chili laughs.

Chili I'm widening horizons – expanding the business. Can't have only
5   you exploiting[232] the riches of this city. When you're done at the college, I'm taking you on as a partner – that's a promise. Between us, we'll hoover up[233] all the money this town's flashing[234] at whoever cares to look. It'll be just like Karachi, being chauffeured in Uncle Asif's Merc[235]. I've got a Beamer, now, five series[236].

10   **Shahid** You need serious cash to have a chauffeur.

Chili Bro, if you can't dream, you won't get. – I need a place to shack[237] in.

Shahid Some of the friends might be using the room for their meetings.

Chili Can't see that big boy staying awake after midnight. She a femi-
15   nist? Bad luck. They tell you your prick[238]'s too small –

Shahid (*interrupting*) How is your wife, by the way?

Chili (*fiercely*[239]) What the hell you saying?

Shahid Just asking after Zulma.

Chili You trying to start me up[240]?

20   **Shahid** No, Chili, I promise.

Chili Sure?

Shahid It was a family enquiry[241].

Chili (*kisses him*) Enjoy, bro. Soon we'll really party. And remember, no one envies[242] another a wank.

25   *Chili exits. Chad enters.*

Chad How is he?

Shahid Who?

Chad Honestly, you are lucky enough to be living here beside him, and you're asking who? Brother Riaz!

---

230   eunuch [' juːnək]: a man who has been castrated
231   Percy Bysshe Shelley ['ʃeli] (1792–1822): major English, Romantic poet
232   to exploit: *ausbeuten*
233   to hoover up (colloquial): to suck in like a vacuum cleaner
234   to flash: to show (money) to impress people
235   Merc: Mercedes
236   Beamer five series: BMW luxury car in the Fiver series
237   to shack: to stay overnight somewhere
238   prick (slang): penis
239   fiercely: aggressively, angrily
240   to start s.o. up (colloquial): to get s.o. angry
241   enquiry: question to obtain information
242   to envy: *beneiden*

Shahid Not bad.

Chad Good, good. There's some project special to his heart he has to complete. I know he'll offer me first look soon – it nearing the end. He's not working too hard?

Shahid shrugs[243].   5

There's a lot to get done.

Shahid What exactly is he working on?

Chad Pardon?

Shahid I mean is there anything more than normal?

Chad He can't talk about it, Shahid.   10

Shahid I know, I know. But –

Chad He up to something[244] with the Iranians, that's all I can say right now. What you said the other day – it touch my heart right through. A man who speaks is like a lion.

A brisk[245] coded knock on the door.   15

They're early.

Chad opens the door to a man carrying a green rucksack, which he holds up to Chad.

Wicked. Ta[246] very much, Zia.

The man drops the rucksack (full of meat cleavers[247], knives, etc.) on the   20
floor, bows[248] and goes away. Chad places the rucksack within reach and
starts rifling through[249] Shahid's clothes.

Shahid What are you doing?

Chad I was thinking, you know, the brother never have time for his-self. He wearing same clothes now for a week. It's important he looks good   25
at the meeting – like a chairman[250]. Or general.

Shahid But Chad –

Chad What now?

Shahid I can't see him in the Fred Perry[251].

Chad No?   30

---

[243] to shrug: to move your shoulders up to show you don't know s.th.
[244] to be up to s.th.: to have s.th. planned
[245] brisk: quick
[246] ta (colloquial, BE): thanks
[247] cleaver: a heavy knife used to cut meat
[248] to bow [baʊ]: to bend the upper part of the body forward
[249] to rifle through: to search quickly through s.th. to find s.th.
[250] chairman: head of a company
[251] Fred Perry: a polo shirt marketed by the English table tennis and tennis player of the same name (1909–1995) in 1952 that later became a favourite with teenagers in the 1960s and 1970s

Shahid And this purple number[252] might make him look effeminate[253].

Chad What?

Shahid Like a poof[254].

Chad That won't do[255]. What you got so many books for?

5 **Shahid** I love reading stories.

Chad How old are you – eight? Aren't there millions of serious things to be done? Out there … it's genocide[256]. Rape[257]. Oppression[258]. Murder. The history of the world is slaughter. And you reading stories like some old grandma.

10 **Shahid** You make it sound like I was shooting up[259] heroin.

Chad Nice one[260].

Shahid But don't writers try to explain that kind of thing? Just now I'm reading **The Possessed**[261] –

Chad What about the dispossessed[262], eh? But let's waste no more time
15 discussing peripheries[263]. We got many real things to accomplish. Hey, where d'you get this Paul Smith[264] shirt?

Shahid (*evasive*[265]) A shop in Brighton[266].

Chad Riaz'll be thrilled[267]. He like Brighton and he look best in red. You big-hearted, too, like a lion. Riaz was right about you.

20 *Another coded knock.*

Now what? Everyone's in a hurry today.

Hat pokes[268] *his head round the door.*

---

252 number: (here): piece of clothing
253 effeminate: looking like a woman
254 poof [pʊf] (slang, BE): homosexual
255 That won't do.: That is not suitable.
256 genocide ['dʒenəsaɪd]: the murder of a whole race or group of people
257 rape: *Vergewaltigung*
258 oppression: *Unterdrückung*
259 to shoot up (slang): to inject a drug directly into the blood
260 nice one: (here): good joke
261 The Possessed: an 1872 political novel by the Russian writer, Fyodor Dostoevsky (1821–1881).
262 dispossesed: those who have had their property taken away, those who have nothing
263 periphery [pə'rɪfəri]: (here): matter of little importance
264 Paul Smith (1946–): British designer and retailer of upscale clothing for men and women that is very traditional with a touch of the unusual
265 evasive: not willing to give clear answers to a question
266 Brighton: famous resort town on the southern coast of England, with large beaches and a great variety of clothing, jewellery, antique shops, restaurants and pubs
267 thrilled: extremely pleased
268 to poke: to push through s.th.

Hat Hey, Shahid, it for you. Popular guy!

Shahid Is it Chili? Say I'm –

Hat A lady.

Zulma strides in.

Zulma Hello, Shahid.   5

Shahid Oh, Zulma Auntie, great to see you. What's up?

Zulma Never call me Auntie, you damn fool. In some quarters I'm a sex
symbol. Here – your ammi asked me to bring your favourite aubergine[269] pakoras.

She hands him the pakoras, wrapped in foil[270] He stashes them away[271]. 10
Chad shuffles[272] out, taking the rucksack and Hat with him.

Shahid She shouldn't have …

Zulma And leave those brain cells unfed? How are the studies coming?

Shahid Fine, fine.

Zulma Working hard?   15

Shahid Never harder.

Zulma Making friends?

Shahid The best ever.

Zulma Have you seen my beloved husband?

Shahid Yes.   20

Zulma When? Where?

Shahid He popped by[273] to say hello.

Zulma That bastard[274] Chili never said hello to anyone. Did he borrow
money? What's his number? My pen is hanging[275]! Where's he staying
at the moment in London? Quickly.   25

Shahid Don't you know?

Zulma I've chucked him out[276] until he cleans up. If he can, or wants to.

Shahid What do you mean, "cleans up?"

Zulma Let's just say your ammi worries about him.

Shahid He's with his friends. Playing poker all night.   30

---

[269] aubergine [ˈəʊbəʒiːn] (BE): (AE) eggplant
[270] foil: thin sheet of metal used for wrapping food
[271] to stash away: to store somewhere safe
[272] to shuffle: to walk slowly without lifting your feet completely off the ground
[273] to pop by (colloquial): to make a short appearance, to visit for a short time
[274] bastard (slang): *Mistkerl*
[275] My pen is hanging!: I've got my pen ready to write down the telephone number.
[276] to chuck s.o. out (colloquial): to throw s.o. out

Zulma What the hell, Shahid, which damn friends? You better tell me or I'll string you up[277] by the balls[278], okay? That brother of yours – Papa's barely got cold and he's off dreaming.

Shahid I must run to the library. You know Chili doesn't tell no one
5   what's what.

Zulma What are you studying?

Shahid Post-colonial literature.

Zulma No finer qualification for a travel agent. Are we still colonial after so long, "post" or not? Get a degree[279] – whatever else, make sure you
10   come out qualified, for your ammi's sake. You haven't got in with a rotten[280] crowd, have you? Intellectuals or some other such fools?

Shahid (*ushering her out*[281]) I've got to hand in an essay tomorrow, Auntie.

Zulma (*forceful*) Shahid! Your ammi is worried. Get Chili to ring her.
15   He hasn't been home for weeks.

Shahid I'll tell him.

Zulma Remember what Papa always said – working your arse off[282] is the only religion worth the name. Do that, and then go home.

Shahid (*ushering her out*) I'll let you know as soon as I hear from Chili,
20   Auntie. Bye.

Zulma exits. Shahid puts the pakoras away and switches on some music as he does his yoga exercises. Chad enters. For a moment, he's entranced[283] by the music.

Chad What you doin'?

25 **Shahid** Yoga. It gets me in the mood.

Chad That Hindu shit will infect your mind.

He turns off the music.

They listen to that Ravi Shankar[284] shit and burn joss sticks[285]. You don't want to end up like George Harrison[286], do you? Shahid, I tell

---

[277] to string up (colloquial): to hang with a rope or string
[278] balls (slang): testicles (*Hoden*)
[279] degree: academic degree (*Grad*)
[280] rotten: terrible, morally corrupt
[281] to usher ['ʌʃə] out: to show s.o. where he or she should or can leave
[282] to work your arse off (slang): to work very hard
[283] entranced: absorbed, captivated, delighted
[284] Ravi Shankar (1920–   ): Indian sitar player
[285] joss stick: incense in the form of a stick, often burned in religious ceremonies
[286] George Harrison (1943–2001): lead guitarist of The Beatles – He became interested in the Hindu religion in the 1960s. He befriended Ravi Shankar and played in a concert with him in 1971.

you, I used to be an addict[287] – a music addict like you. I listened to it day and night! It was overtaking my soul!

Shahid You were controlled by music?

Chad I'm talking of the music and fashion industries. Telling us what to wear, where to go, what to listen to. Ain't we their slaves? 5

Shahid I'm not living without music. Tell me the truth – you miss it too.

Chad (*pointed*)[288] Don't you want to swim in a clean sea and see by a clear light? Imagine the warm water holding you up!

He hugs Shahid.

Are we dancing monkeys? We have minds and sense. Gimme[289] those 10 Prince records!

Shahid Some of them are imports!

Chad Allah is the only one we must submit to! He put our noses on our face –

Shahid As opposed to[290] where? 15

Chad Our stomach, for instance. How can you deny his skill and power and authority?

Shahid I don't, Chad, you know I don't. And you know I respect you as a brother too, that's why I'm asking you to stop!

Chad We think we cool but we break our trust with Allah. Listen to 20 Riaz. Don't he say we becoming Western, European, Socialist? We must not assimilate, that way we lose our souls. Like that blaspheming writer! We are proud and we are obedient[291]. It's not we who must change, but the world!

Shahid Here – keys to paradise. Have a good meeting. 25

As he's about to leave, Tahira enters.

Chad This wonderful sister is Tahira.

Chad picks up the foil-wrapped parcel[292] Shahid stashed away.

Shahid (*to Tahira*) Hi. Did you meet my aunt on her way out?

Tahira (*holding his hand*) That air hostess[293] wear sunglasses to hide her 30 evil eye! Don't worry – we all have auntie problems. One day all aunties will be under our control.

Shahid leaves, as people begin to gather to meet Riaz. Music. Shahid makes his way through night-time London to Deedee's.

---

[287] addict: (here): a person unable to stop doing s.th.
[288] pointed: directed or intended for a particular person
[289] gimme (slang): give me
[290] As opposed to where?: Instead of where else?
[291] obedient [əˈbiːdiənt]: willing to obey, doing as you are told
[292] parcel: something wrapped up, package
[293] air hostess: stewardess

47

SCENE FIVE

Deedee's house. Night. Deedee has had a row[294] with Brownlow. He storms off[295] into the bedroom. Shahid enters.

Shahid Thanks for inviting me to look at the Prince videos. I wouldn't
5   be able to write my Prince paper without it. Where are the others?
Deedee I'll heat some soup while you watch.
Deedee goes to the kitchen. Shahid watches the video. He is emulating Prince's moves, gestures[296], etc., when Deedee returns.
   Find him sexy?
10 *Shahid quickly checks his notebook.*
Shahid His work is ... seamless[297] ... seamless and not a little cathartic[298], wouldn't you say?
Deedee I hate this fucking house.
Shahid Pardon?
15 **Deedee** We're trying to sell it. Sorry, what did you say?
Enter Brownlow, putting on his tie[299]. Stops on seeing Shahid. He holds out his hand.
Brownlow H-h-hello, Tariq. I'm Andrew Brownlow.
Shahid I'm Shahid.
20 **Brownlow** O-o-of course. Extra lessons, hmm?
Shahid (*agreeing*) Prince.
Brownlow Charles?
Shahid No, the sex symbol.
Brownlow Of course. F. R. Leavis[300] would be reassured[301] and so would
25   Queenie[302].
Shahid Who?
Brownlow What?

---

[294] row [raʊ]: argument
[295] to storm off: to leave angrily
[296] gesture: movement of body, hands or head to communicate s.th.
[297] seamless: *nahtlos*
[298] cathartic: having the quality of relieving or reducing tension, originating from the Greek philosopher Aristotle's definition of a tragedy
[299] tie: *Kravatte*
[300] Frank Raymond Leavis (1895–1978): major British literary critic, husband of Queenie Leavis
[301] to reassure: to say or do s.th. that makes s.o. less frightened or worried
[302] Queenie: Queenie Dorothy Leavis (1906–1981): an English literary critic and essayist with a special interest for the English, European, and American novel

48

Shahid Queenie?

Brownlow It's true I'm not feeling that heterosexual at the moment. (*to Deedee*) W-w-well. S-s-see you. B-b-bye.

Deedee (*cutting him off*) Yes, all right, see you tomorrow.

He leaves. 5

"Yes" is a lovely word. I love "yes." Yes, yes, yes. No victims, no victors, just "yes."

Shahid My brother Chili lives by the word –

Deedee It was discovered in South America. Chilli[303] only came to India in medieval times[304]. 10

Shahid I didn't know that. We're from Pakistan.

Deedee Once, years ago, Andrew came home from a party and described kissing a woman.

Shahid Dr Brownlow?

Deedee I had never felt so let down[305] – couldn't sleep for two nights. You 15 would hope that intimacy[306] would leave more of a mark. But now I think, who is this person? I want a smoke.

Shahid (*apologetic[307]*) I don't smoke.

She shows him a spliff[308].

Whoa[309]! I've only smoked that once before. In Brighton. 20

Deedee Enjoy it?

Shahid The person who gave it me said I should come and see you.

Deedee Well. ...! What do you say? It'll make you laugh.

Shahid It's okay, I laughed earlier. Could you have a look at this?

Offers his rolled-up manuscript. 25

Deedee Interesting ...

Shahid You haven't read it yet.

Deedee Give me a few years.

Shahid Thanks. (*Quickly, referring to[310] the spliff.*) I want it.

Deedee Sure? 30

---

[303] chilli: Deedee is referring to chilli pepper that indeed originated in South America, but spread to Europe and India after Christopher Columbus' discovery of the New World at the end of the 15th century.

[304] medieval times: *Mittelalter*

[305] let down: disappointed

[306] intimacy: close, personal relationship with s.o. that might also be sexual in nature

[307] apologetic: showing you are sorry for having done s.th. wrong

[308] spliff (slang, BE): a cigarette with marijuana

[309] Whoa! [wəʊ]: expression used to show great surprise

[310] to refer to: to draw s.o.'s attention to s.th.

Shahid takes it, draws[311] mightily and passes it on.

Shahid What is this?

Deedee Moroccan.

Shahid takes his leather jacket off.

5   What're you doing?

Shahid Feeling good, too.

She starts laughing.

What?

Deedee If my friends could see me now …! Kids, mortgages[312], this would
10   not even register[313] in their dreams! What do you want to do when you
grow up?

She turns up the music while Shahid takes another long draw.

Shahid (*affecting[314] a Chili-like nonchalance[315]*) Whatever you want me
to do, babe[316].

15 **Deedee** Yes, call me baby[317]. Baby, baby, baby.

She starts moving to the music, slowly, while Shahid watches her dance.

Can't wait to get a place of my own.

Shahid Why are you splitting up[318]?

Deedee For years I was involved with his politics. Too involved. It all
20   makes you feel guilty. It limits the imagination.

Shahid What d'you like now?

Deedee (*holding up the spliff*) This. Teaching. Music. When I can, I do
a lot of nothing. And make stabs at[319] pleasure. (*Pops open a pill box.*)
Want one?

25 **Shahid** What are they?

Deedee E. Ecstasy. It'll make you see around corners.

Shahid Is this why you invited me over?

Deedee No. Because you're lonely and I like the way you look at me.

Shahid pops[320] a pill. She offers him a bottle of water to swig[321] with the
30 *pill and resumes dancing, after popping one herself.*

---

[311] to draw: to breathe in
[312] mortgage ['mɔːgɪdʒ]: *Hypothek*
[313] to register: to notice, to be aware of, to make an impression
[314] to affect: (here): to imitate
[315] nonchalance: indifference, giving the impression you are relaxed and calm
[316] babe (slang): a way of addressing a young, attractive girl
[317] baby (slang): an affectionate way of addressing a young woman
[318] to split up: to stop having a relationship with s.o.
[319] to make a stab at s.th.: to make an attempt to do s.th.
[320] to pop (slang): to take a pill
[321] to swig: to drink deeply from a bottle

You've got *cafe-au-lait*[322] skin.
She recites[323].
    A savage[324] place! As holy[325] and enchanted[326].
    As e'er[327] beneath[328] a waning[329] moon was haunted[330].
    By woman wailing[331] for her demon[332] lover!   5
Shahid (*continuing the rhyme from "Kubla Khan*[333]*"*)
    And from this chasm[334], with ceaseless[335] turmoil[336] seething[337],
    As if this earth in fast thick pants[338] were breathing,
    A mighty fountain[339] momently was forced!
Deedee, impressed, acknowledges Shahid's participation. She listlessly[340] 10
flicks through[341] *his manuscript.*
Deedee Tell me your story …
Shahid draws more on his spliff and pops another pill.
Shahid Everybody's free, everybody's free with Prince on the gas[342]!

---

[322] café-au-lait (French): light brown like coffee with milk
[323] to recite: to say a poem or piece of literature you have learned by heart
[324] savage: wild, uncivilised
[325] holy: *heilig*
[326] enchanted: *verzaubert*
[327] e'er (poetic): ever
[328] beneath: under
[329] to wane: to decrease in size, to become smaller
[330] to haunt: to visit a place in the form of a ghost
[331] to wail [weɪl]: to make a long, loud, high cry because you are sad or in pain
[332] demon ['diːmən]: evil spirit
[333] Kubla Khan: poem by the English Romantic poet Samuel Taylor Coleridge (1772–1834), completed in 1797 and published in 1816 – According to Coleridge's Preface to Kubla Khan, the poem was composed one night after he experienced an opium-influenced dream after reading a work describing the Tartar king Kublai Khan. The poem also presents the Orient as something strange and mysterious. It begins:
In Xanadu did Kubla Khan
A stately pleasure-dome decree:
Where Alph, the sacred river, ran
Through caverns measureless to man
Down to a sunless sea
[334] chasm ['kæzm]: abyss, deep opening in the ground
[335] ceaseless: constant
[336] turmoil: violent or confused motion
[337] to seethe: to boil or foam
[338] pant: act of breathing noisily and deeply
[339] fountain: strong flow of water forced into the air
[340] listlessly: without energy or enthusiasm
[341] to flick through: to quickly turn the pages
[342] with Prince on the gas (slang): listening to Prince while high on drugs

Deedee Cold, wet and worthy[343] – that's all Greenham Common[344] amounted to[345].

Shahid I read Shelley to her, sitting by the pond. Papa was so mad.

Deedee Dress like a punk and leave home …

5 *Shahid pops another pill while Deedee resumes[346] dancing.*

Let's go to the end-of-decade[347] party!

Shahid The decade hasn't ended yet.

Deedee It will feel like it has! See how the under-classes are fighting back against Thatcher's greed[348]."

10 *She grabs Shahid and they rush out of the door. Strapper is seen dealing drugs to some students on the road. Shahid and Deedee go along with them, shouting "End-of-decade party!"*

Rave[349] music. Shadows coalesce[350] into a rave scene[351].

SCENE SIX

15 *Shahid's digs. Shahid returns. Preparing for bed, he retches[352] and falls. Riaz, disturbed by the noise, comes into his room, and is alarmed to see Shahid choking on[353] his vomit[354]. He picks him up and lays him to bed. Pulls down his trousers and covers him with a blanket.*

Confused, Shahid calls out Riaz's name. The latter[355] hushes[356] him to
20 *sleep.*

---

343 worthy: having qualities that deserve your respect, attention or admiration
344 Greenham Common: military airfield 80 km west of London, used by the Royal Air Force and the American Air Corps during WW II and by the American Air Force during the Cold War – In the 1980s and 1990s it was the site of protests by women who created the Greenham Common Women's Peace Camp to demand the removal of Cruise missiles that had nuclear warheads.
345 to amount to: to add up to
346 to resume: to begin again with s.th.
347 end-of-the-decade: i.e., the late 1980s
348 greed: *Gier*
349 rave: electronic dance music
350 to coalesce [ˌkəʊəˈles]: to merge, to blend, to fuse, to come together
351 rave scene: an organised party with electronic dance music held in a field or abandoned building often with drugs
352 to retch: to vomit *(sich erbrechen)*
353 to choke on s.th.: to be unable to breathe because the passage to your lungs is blocked by s.th.
354 vomit: the food that comes out of the mouth when vomiting
355 the latter: the second person or thing mentioned
356 to hush: to make s.o. become quieter by speaking softly

When he sees Shahid finally asleep, he recites[357] *a prayer, cleans the room and slips out*[358].

SCENE SEVEN

Shahid's digs. Morning. Shahid's lying on his bed, groggy[359]. *Chad enters, excited. Riaz is a pace*[360] *behind, carrying a folder bearing*[361] *his manu-*   5
script, with Tahira in tow[362].

Chad You're definitely the lucky type. The brother asked for you particularly.
Shahid mumbles[363] *incoherently*[364].
Riaz How are you feeling, Shahid?   10
Shahid continues to mumble.
Chad Shahid!
Shahid Huh[365]? What is it?
Riaz Please.
He places the folder in Shahid's hand.   15
Chad (*bending over Shahid and reading the cover page*) "The Martyr's[366] Imagination" …?
Riaz Yes. It is my little book.
Tahira (*excited*) It's finished?
Riaz Pen-written only until now.   20
Tahira Is it an attack on that blaspheming writer?
Riaz (*continuing, to Shahid*) Please, would you do one thing for me?
Shahid Whatever you want, Riaz.
Riaz Will you convert it to print?
Shahid Of course.   25
Riaz Many others have volunteered but you are the right person for this task.

---

[357] to recite: to say a poem, prayer, or piece of literature you have learned by heart
[358] to slip out: to leave quietly and quickly
[359] groggy: weak and unable to think properly because of being tired
[360] pace: step
[361] to bear: (here): to contain
[362] in tow [təʊ]: following close behind
[363] to mumble: to speak softly in a way that is difficult to understand
[364] incoherently: in a disorganised way
[365] huh [hʌ]: *Was?*
[366] martyr ['mɑ:tə]: *Märtyrer, -in*

Shahid listlessly looks through the manuscript.

I am from a small village in Pakistan. They are basically ... songs of memory, adolescence[367] and twilight[368]. But perhaps they will change the world a little, too.

5 **Shahid** I didn't know you –

Riaz It's God's work.

Shahid With your name on the title page.

Riaz *(laughing)* Yes, I am entirely to blame.

Tahira *(to Riaz)* What message does the book have, brother?

10 **Riaz** *(holding her face tenderly[369])* The message – and all good art must have a message – is of love and compassion[370].

Chad Beautiful.

Shahid Brother Riaz, thank you, thank you for everything!

Riaz No, no.

15 *Riaz and Tahira leave.*

Chad Wow, that's incredible! I offer you one warning – you must be strictly confidential[371] about this.

Shahid Are you saying I'm not trustworthy[372]?

Chad No, no, brother. But many important people in the community
20 wouldn't like him being too creative. It too frivolous[373] for them. Some of those guys go into a supermarket and if music playing, they run out again. Why don't you enjoy some rest before you begin such important work?

Shahid lies down, Chad reads the manuscript.

25 *(Reading.)* Magnificent, "Gibreel's[374] fragrant[375] green sword will veil[376] the unveiled ..."

Shahid sits up and reaches for the bowl beside his bed.

---

[367] adolescence: puberty

[368] twilight ['twaɪlaɪt]: time just after sunset, or (fig.): the last phase of a person's life

[369] tenderly: gently

[370] compassion: sympathy for people who are suffering and the desire to help them

[371] confidential: not telling others about a secret

[372] trustworthy: reliable, honest, dependable

[373] frivolous: silly, not serious in attitude or behaviour

[374] Gibreel [dʒiˈbriːl] (Gabriel): Muslims believe Gabriel to have been the angel who revealed the Qur'an to the prophet Muhammad.

[375] fragrant ['freɪgrənt]: having a pleasant smell

[376] to veil [veɪl]: to cover with a veil *(Schleier)*

"Wet bodies and captivating[377] tongues reek of[378] Satan[379]'s hot breath, Gibreel's fragrant green sword …"

Shahid whimpers[380].

    You know, Shahid brother, there's something else Riaz wants you to do. He was shy of[381] asking you, I know.   5

Shahid What is it?

Chad He needs your help to get the book published.

Shahid retches into the bowl.

Shahid He saved my life.

Chad He intuitive – you owe him the lot.   10

Shahid I'll do whatever I can to repay him.

Chad You'll help him find a publisher for the book?

Shahid Sure.

Tahira bursts in[382], followed by Hat and an Old Man.

Tahira We need clear space here. (*to Shahid*) You going to help or lie 15 there all day?

Shahid What now?

Shahid gets up wearily[383]. He is in his underpants. Tahira looks at him, then Hat positions himself to hide Shahid from her view. She seats the Old Man on a chair. Riaz comes in.   20

    Hat (*to Shahid*) Now you'll hear something about how nice your little England is.

Riaz makes the Old Man sit at ease[384] and listens attentively[385].

Old Man These boys, please, sir, are coming into my flat and threatening my whole family every day and night. They have punched[386] me in my 25 stomach, spit all the time at[387] my wife when she goes out for shopping, make rude[388] signs at my daughters when they go to school. Five years I have lived there, but it is getting worse. I am afraid.

Riaz (*considers[389]*) What do you suggest we do to help, Shahid?

---

[377] captivating: fascinating
[378] to reek of: to smell of s.th. in a very unpleasant way
[379] Satan ['seɪtn]
[380] to whimper: to cry, to sob, to whine softly
[381] to be shy of doing s.th.: to be afraid of doing s.th.
[382] to burst in: to suddenly enter a room
[383] wearily: in a very tired manner
[384] at ease: relaxed, comfortable
[385] attentively: carefully
[386] to punch: to hit s.o. or s.th. hard with your fist
[387] to spit at: *jdn. anspucken*
[388] rude: impolite, showing no respect
[389] to consider: to think about s.th. carefully before making a decision

Shahid (*offhand*[390]) Teach the beggars[391] a lesson.

Riaz Excellent. We're not blasted[392] Christians. We don't turn the other buttock[393]. We will fight for our people who are being tortured any-where – in Palestine, Afghanistan, Kashmir, East End[394]! (*To the Old Man, reassuring, as he ushers him out.*) Action will be taken very soon. That is my promise to you.

Old Man exits.

Tahira Self-defence is no offence[395].

Shahid What are you talking about?

Riaz We want you with us tonight, Shahid.

Chad Shahid's always with us.

Shahid I have to see someone on family business later – after working on your poem …

Riaz Work on the poem can wait. It is our duty to make sure this man can feel free again.

Chad No degradation[396] of our people. Anybody who fails to fight will answer to God and hellfire!

Shahid I'll be punished if I don't take part?

Riaz Punishment is only for those who degrade our people. I've written a poem on this subject. "The Wrath[397]." Have you reached it yet?

Shahid Which one? Is it at the end?

Riaz No! It's the second one – "The Wrath." "The Wrath."

Shahid No, not yet. (*Sarky[398].*) Why not call ourselves the Foreign Legion[399]?

Chad I knew you were with us.

He picks up the holdall[400].

---

[390] offhand: without care or thought

[391] beggar (colloquial): fellow

[392] blasted (slang): *verflucht*

[393] buttock: *Hinterbacke* – Cf. the idea of turning the other cheek in Matthew 5:38–42 and Luke 6:27–31

[394] East End: area of London to the east and north characterised by poverty and a large immigration population, in the last 40 years especially Bangladeshi people

[395] offence: crime, unlawful act

[396] degradation: the act of treating s.o. with no respect, mistreatment

[397] wrath [rɒθ]: extreme anger

[398] sarky (colloquial, BE): sarcastic

[399] Foreign Legion: a body of foreign volunteers serving in an army, especially that of France

[400] holdall (BE): a large handbag made of cloth or soft leather

This is it, brothers and sisters. Grab[401] something warm to wear, Shahid – it be chilly[402] in the East End.

Tahira (*chanting*[403]) Foreign Legion! Foreign Legion!

Hat (*picking up the chant*) Foreign Legion! Foreign Legion!

As they leave, Chili enters. 5

Chili Hello – where's the bad posse[404] headed to?

Chad (*to Shahid*) Catch you outside.

Chad, Riaz, Hat and Tahira leave.

Chili (*to Shahid*) What shit you getting into, bro[405]?

Shahid Nothing. 10

Chili Where's my Paul Smith?

Shahid What?

Chili The red Paul Smith shirt I gave you.

Shahid (*quickly*) You won't believe it – coming back from Deedee's last night – 15

Chili You did her?[406]

Shahid Met some of her students who were off to an end-of-decade party – took me to this rave in a white house out of town. Man, Ecstasy was flowing like confetti. I had your famous King's Road[407] sandwich[408] – shagged[409] three girls who I didn't even know – puked[410] all over the red 20 Paul Smith I was wearing and had to take it to the laundrette –

Chili You shitting me?[411]

Shahid No, I swear, Chili. I wore it to impress her up, like you said.

Chili (*suddenly hugging*[412] *him*) I'm proud of you, baby bro. Papa will be smiling up in paradise. 25

Shahid Business okay?

Chili Why?

---

[401] to grab: to take s.th. with your hand, firmly and quickly

[402] chilly: unpleasantly cold

[403] to chant: to sing or shout the same words or phrases many times

[404] posse ['pɒsi] (USA): in the past, especially in the West: a group of people assembled together by a sheriff in order to help him catch a criminal

[405] bro (colloquial): brother

[406] You did her?: You had sex with her?

[407] King's Road: main street in Chelsea, west London that was the location of the hippie and punk counterculture, and sexual liberation in the 1960s and 1970s

[408] sandwich (slang): having sex with two women at the same time

[409] to shag (slang, BE): to have sex with s.o.

[410] to puke (colloquial): to vomit

[411] You shitting me? (slang): Are you telling me the truth?

[412] to hug: to put your arms around s.o. as a sign of affection

Shahid I may not get back tonight –

Chili Still haven't told me what shit[413] you're getting into.

Shahid I've got to rush – they'll be waiting …

Chili (*fierce*[414]) I'm your brother, for Christ sakes!

5 **Shahid** I'm helping some people out, that's all. It's a charity[415] thing.

Chili (*dismissive*[416]) Charity! You're still a baby, bro. There's only one thing that matters in the world, that's number one[417] and money. Got myself a partner to keep an eye out for supplies while I meet demands[418] of my varied customers.

10 **Shahid** What work are you really doing? Zulma came round.

Chili What you tell her?

Shahid You were at friends playing poker.

Chili Good boy!

Shahid She chuck you out[419]?

15 **Chili** Temporary[420] loss of facilities[421], as they say in the trade[422].

Shahid You're the golden couple of Sevenoaks.

Chili laughs.

(*Insistent*[423].) Go home.

Chili You can't never go back home.

20 **Shahid** Ring Ammi at least.

Chili (*admonishing*[424]) Don't they teach you respect at college?

Shahid I've got to go.

He leaves Chili looking around the room. Chili sees the copy of **The Satanic Verses**, *flicks through*[425] *it nonchalantly*[426]*, then shuts the book*

---

413 shit (slang): trouble

414 fierce: angrily and aggressively

415 charity: an activity to help s.o. in need with money, clothes, etc.

416 dismissive: showing you don't believe a person or thing to be important

417 number one: (here): yourself

418 meet demands of varied customers: make sure that various customers get what they desire, especially drugs – Cf. the law of supply and demand *(Angebot und Nachfrage)*

419 to chuck s.o. out (colloquial, BE): to throw out

420 temporary: lasting for a short time

421 facilities (plural): (ironic): buildings, services, equipment for a particular purpose – (here): home

422 in the trade (ironic): in the business world

423 insistent: demanding s.th. firmly and refusing to accept any opposition

424 to admonish: to reprove *(ermahnen)*

425 to flick through: to turn the pages quickly without reading everything

426 nonchalantly: in an unconcerned or indifferent way

and lays out a line[427] of coke[428]. After snorting[429], stuffs[430] his remaining stash[431] in the book and puts it away carefully.
Music, as Shahid and the gang, carrying rucksacks, make their way to the East End flat.

SCENE EIGHT

5

A high-rise flat in the East End. Night. The gang tip out[432] knives, cleavers, etc. from the rucksacks they've been carrying.

Chad Weapons training.
Chad demonstrates, to the accompaniment of rousing[433] quwaali[434] music from his boom box[435]. Shahid, Hat and Tahira go through a drill[436]. Chad 10
starts to weep[437].
Shahid What's wrong, Chad?
Chad I'm moved by my people's suffering. Can't keep it together[438].
Shahid If you keep blubbing[439], the old man is not going to have much
    confidence[440] in us.   15
Chad You're right. (*Blows his nose.*) You stubborn[441] but sensible. We
    here to defend the man terrorised by racists. Bring 'em on![442] United
    in defence of West Compton Estate[443]!

---

[427] line: thin and narrow layer
[428] coke (slang): cocaine
[429] to snort (slang): to take drugs by breathing them in through the nose
[430] to stuff: to push s.th. quickly into a small space
[431] stash (slang): drugs
[432] to tip out: to remove s.th. from a bag or container by moving one side higher than
    the other
[433] rousing: full of energy and enthusiasm
[434] quwaali: a form of Sufi religious music popular in South Asia, particularly in areas
    with a strong Muslim presence, such as Pakistan, Punjab, Sindh, Hyderabad and
    parts of North India
[435] boom box (BE): large portable radio and cassette player that can play loud music
[436] drill: repeated exercises to learn s.th.
[437] to weep, wept, wept: to cry because of being sad
[438] Can't keep it together. (colloquial): I can't control myself emotionally.
[439] to blub (colloquial, BE): to cry
[440] confidence: feeling that you can trust s.o.
[441] stubborn: refusing to change your mind or opinion
[442] Bring 'em on! (colloquial): Let them attack us! We're ready for them!
[443] estate (BE): area of housing built by the local government for people with low
    incomes – West Compton Estate does not actually exist.

They finish their drill. Tahira clears a study area for Hat as the guys lounge[444] *after the work out. Shahid looks*[445] *to slip away but Chad holds him back.*

(*To Shahid, watching Tahira at work.*) This great sister here, Tahira, she been with us from day one. Riaz like a father to her. Her old man threw her out because she wanted her mum and sisters to cover up[446].

Tahira Park yourself[447] here, Hat.

Hat Ta[448], Tahira.

He moves to the space Tahira's cleared for him, takes out his books from his duffel bag[449] *and starts on his homework. Tahira sits with the others.*

Tahira (*to Shahid*) Hat always studying. His father – he's putting too much pressure on him to be an accountant.

Shahid He's here with us tonight.

Tahira But the father thinks Hat visiting his auntie in Sunderland[450] today.

Chad He think we stopping Hat being an accountant. But we ain't. We only say accountants have to meet many women. And shake hands with them. They expected, too, to take alcohol every day and get involved in interest[451] payments. We not sure Hat won't feel left out, you know?

Tahira And you're expected to take drugs in the City. And meet strippers at lunchtime. Chad, could you close your legs, please?

Chad brings his knees together.

Tahira I see you like wearing tight trousers.

Chad I do, yes.

Tahira Can't you wear something looser? We have to look modest[452]. Think it's easy wearing the hijab[453]? Yesterday a man on the street ripped my scarf off and shouted, "This is England, not Arabia."

---

[444] to lounge [laʊndʒ]: to sit or stand around in a relaxed manner
[445] looks: (here): tries
[446] to cover up: (here): to wear a scarf or veil
[447] to park yourself (colloquial): to sit or stand somewhere
[448] ta (slang, BE): thank you
[449] duffel bag: a long, round bag made out of cloth closed by a string around the top
[450] Sunderland: port in north-east England
[451] interest: *Zinsen*
[452] modest ['mɒdɪst]: *bescheiden*
[453] hijab [hɪ'dʒɑːb] (Arabic): a covering for the face or head worn by some Muslim women

Chad (*sheepish[454], looking at Shahid*) I've been looking out for some Oxford bags[455] for a while.

Tahira That will be progress. And aren't you thinking of growing a beard? Look at Hat, his is really coming on now. (*Feeling Shahid's smooth-shaven chin.*) Even Shahid has got something bushy on the way. 5

Chad My skin needs breathing space, otherwise I develop an itchy[456] rash[457].

Tahira Vanity[458] should be the least of your concerns[459].

Chad (*to Shahid*) I'll put something bushy in your face if you don't stop 10 smirkin'[460]!

Shahid Sorry, brother. How long is this vigil[461] going to last?

Chad Could be days, you know – them racists sometimes clever.

Shahid I have to go off for a few hours – family business.

Just as Shahid is about to leave, Riaz enters, wearing the red Paul Smith 15 *shirt and jeans. The gang stare at him.*

Chad All present, brother Riaz.

Riaz I am very happy you are with us, Shahid.

Shahid (*appraising[462] Riaz*) Suits[463] you.

Riaz is puzzled. Chad steps in to explain. 20

Chad (*to Riaz*) Your clothes needed washing, brother. Shahid lent his shirt and trousers. (*With pride.*) Brother Riaz look smart, eh!

Riaz Thank you. Thank you. (*Diffident[464].*) I just picked up what I saw on my chair – fashion passes by me[465].

Tahira You look like a general. 25

Chad Or a chairman. When the racists see the brothers strong, they whimper like dogs with tails between their legs!

Riaz Time for prayers.

---

[454] sheepish: feeling embarrassed because you have done s.th. or said s.th. that is silly

[455] Oxford bags (BE): loose-fitting baggy form of trousers worn by Oxford students from the 1920s to 1950s that again became popular in the 1970s in Great Britain, often with platform shoes

[456] itchy: *juckend*

[457] rash: *Ausschlag*

[458] vanity: too much pride in your appearance

[459] concern: s.th. to worry about

[460] to smirk: to smile in a silly or unpleasant manner

[461] vigil: a purposeful watch, especially at night, to guard s.th.

[462] to appraise: to examine s.o. or s.th. to form an opinion

[463] to suit: to make s.o. look good or attractive (said of clothing)

[464] diffident: lacking self-confidence, shy, timid

[465] passes by me: (correct English): passes me by: is of no interest to me

There is a loud bang[466] on the door. Startled, they pick up their weapons, as Chad pushes Shahid forward.

Chad Check it out. Don't fear – you reinforced up[467]!

Shahid opens the door and sees an eager[468] Strapper, looking around curiously.

Strapper Want anything?

Shahid What?

Strapper Skunk[469], trips[470], E[471]? Don't worry, all the Paki-busters[472] are indoors watching the match.

Shahid Show us where they live, then. You know who they are.

Strapper What're you gonna do, burn them out? I can fire places up[473], if you like.

Shahid Who are you?

Strapper Strapper. An Asian family left their flat and I'm squatting[474] here for my business.

Shahid What business?

Strapper You name it, man, I've had experience of it. Police, courts, kids' homes, rehabilitation centres, social workers. I tell you, Blacks and Pakis, the people put down, and outside[475], they generous and loving. My partner – he a Paki like you – he takes me to all kinds of hip[476] apartments in his cool car, full of birds[477]. Keeps saying this place's too small for him. If you're not buying nothing, I gotta[478] swing over to him in north London – our new base of operations!

Shahid Where are the racists, Strapper? Just point at their door and we'll do the rest.

Strapper laughs.

---

[466] bang: hard blow or knock
[467] reinforced up: (correct English): reinforced: supported by more weapons and people
[468] eager: very excited and interested in what is about to happen
[469] skunk (slang): cannabis
[470] trip: any drug that causes hallucinations such as LSD
[471] E (slang): ecstasy
[472] Paki-buster (slang): racist who likes to beat up Pakistanis
[473] to fire up (colloquial): to start a fire in a building
[474] to squat (colloquial): to live in a building without the owner's permission
[475] put down, and outside: oppressed by those in power and forced to live at the edge of society
[476] hip: trendy
[477] bird (slang, BE): young woman
[478] gotta (slang): have got to

Strapper You wanna[479] find someone who hates another race? Just knock on any door. Course[480] I used to be a skinhead, myself.

Shahid What?

Strapper Supported Millwall[481], see. Me[482] Black mates were always chasing me. One time they tied a noose[483] round me neck and tried to throw me over a bridge. 5

Shahid drags him back into the flat. Frosty[484] atmosphere.

Shahid This is Strapper. Maybe he can help.

Strapper How you doing, Trevor, mate? Respect, eh?

Chad Fuck off[485]! That's not my truth! 10

Strapper Just being polite.

Chad (*to Shahid*) What the fuck[486] you bring him here for?

Strapper You a Paki, me a delinquent[487]. How does it feel to be a problem for this world?

Chad (*pushing Strapper*) I'm a solution, not a problem! Diseases like you 15 need sterilising.

Strapper Don't touch me, man – I got rights too, you know.

Shahid (*to Chad*) He could point out the racists – we'd seize the initiative then.

Chad He can only point to his arse[488]. We got our sister here to think 20 of.

Tahira Chad can be fierce when his blood races.

Brownlow rushes in.

Brownlow Comrades! Any sign of the lunatics[489]?

Strapper Not till now! 25

Riaz welcomes Brownlow in.

Riaz We are so happy you received the message and are able to provide support, Dr Brownlow. So many immoral people surround us here.

---

[479] wanna (slang): want to
[480] course (colloquial): of course
[481] Millwall: Millwall Football Club in south-east London
[482] me (colloquial, BE): my
[483] noose: *Schlinge*
[484] frosty: very unfriendly
[485] Fuck off! (slang): Go away!
[486] what the fuck (slang): why the hell
[487] delinquent: a young person who tends to commit crimes
[488] arse (slang, BE): the part of the body you sit on
[489] lunatic: crazy person

Brownlow Ghastly[490] – this estate! What has been done to these people! Crimes against humanity. Important to visit wastelands[491] regularly. Lest[492] we forget. Seeing them, one understands a lot. It's obvious, not surprising –

5 **Riaz** I beg your pardon? What is not surprising to you, Dr Brownlow, my friend?

Brownlow is leering at[493] Tahira. She moves closer to Hat.

Brownlow That they're violently in love with beauty. I've been wading[494] around, you know, an hour or two in Hades[495], lost in the foul[496]
10 damp[497]. Breeding grounds[498] of race antipathy[499] – infecting everyone, passed on like Aids. Often wished in my adult life, that I could be r-r-religious.

Riaz It is never too late for higher wisdom.

Brownlow (*apologetic*[500]) Read Bertrand Russell[501] at fourteen. Expect
15 you know him, don't you, T-T-Tariq?

Shahid My name is Shahid.

Brownlow Of course. Does Deedee only make you watch Prince videos?

Shahid She's a good teacher.

20 **Brownlow** Not a patch on Russell[502], I bet. Put the deity[503] in his place, Russell. Said that if He existed He would be a fool. God is man's greatest creation. (*To Riaz*) Surely the act of believing is – of no practical use on these estates, to this class. It – it is – dishonest! Yes, d-d-dishonest!
25 Even the lowest class must decide good and evil for themselves.

---

490 ghastly (mostly upper-class use): terrible
491 wasteland: area of land that is not or cannot be used – Cf. the poem, *The Waste Land* by T. S. Eliot (1888–1965)
492 lest (formal): in case
493 to leer at: to look at or smile at s.o. in an unpleasant way because of sexual interest
494 to wade: to walk with effort through mud or water
495 Hades ['heɪdiːz] (Greek mythology): the land of the dead
496 foul[faʊl]: dirty and smelling bad
497 damp: *Feuchtigkeit*
498 breeding ground (fig.): a place where s.th. bad can develop
499 antipathy [æn'tɪpəθi]: strong feeling of dislike
500 apologetic: showing you are sorry for having done s.th. wrong
501 Bertrand Russell (1872–1970): British philosopher and mathematician known for his pacifist views
502 not a patch on Russell (colloquial, BE): not nearly as good as Russell
503 the deity (formal): God

Riaz Please excuse me, but you are a little arrogant. First you ask these poor people to believe in the brotherhood of classes. Now, when your Communist dream has been shown to be just that, you set them adrift[504] to think for themselves. You see now how Western civilisation is proving to be a hoax[505]? 5

Brownlow But this civilisation has also brought us –

Strapper Drugs, mate – and the police.

Brownlow (*ignoring the interruption*) – science, psychoanalysis, a stable political culture, organised sport – at a pretty high level, mind you, e-e-except for England. And all this hand in hand with critical en- 10 quiry[506]. Which means steely[507] questions. And ideas. Ideas being the e-e-enemy of religion.

Riaz Why must they be? My dear Dr Brownlow, revolution everywhere has been an act of faith[508].

Brownlow No – that is how the working classes have been exploited. More 15 than any other class they must be f-f-free to think for themselves.

Riaz And what did free thinking bring them with your Communism? The great gift we offer our poor uneducated – (*indicating[509] Strapper*) yes, even this uneducated poor boy – is the example of our Prophet – peace be upon him! – who brought about a revolution of equality in 20 Arabia by the simple act of belief.

Brownlow I must admit not having associated revolution with I-I-Islam. I suspect that is what F-F-Foucault[510] discovered in the Iranian revolution in '79.

Riaz I do not know the man personally, my friend, but he sounds like a 25 good man whose heart has been changed by simple belief. And don't we all strive[511] to be good?

Brownlow Foucault saw in the revolution a clear triumph of the Iranian working class.

Riaz Precisely what we can achieve here. Come now, it is time to pray. I 30 will be your guide.

---

504 to set s.o. adrift (fig.): to allow s.o. to continue to live without any goal or purpose
505 hoax: joke, trick
506 enquiry: the act of seeking answers
507 steely: determined, firm
508 act of faith: *Vertrauenssache*
509 to indicate: to show with your hand or head
510 Michel Foucault ['fu:kəʊ] (1926–1984): French philosopher and historian, who supported the Iranian revolution of 1979
511 to strive: to try very hard to achieve s.th.

Strapper leaves. Riaz unfurls[512] his prayer mat and kneels on it. The others clear space and follow his example. Shahid stands awkwardly[513] by, before Hat guides him. The "azaan[514]" is heard. When they finish, Riaz sits, with the others fanned[515] around him.

5   Now I am calm. So, my subject today. Adam and Eve, not Adam and Steve[516].

Laughter.

Allah in his mercy has given us another sign of his continuing magnificence, through the disease that has now taken over the West – Aids. A
10 name through which Allah reveals[517] his warning – Adam is definitely Satan! For it is when Adam and Steve come together that the West is shown by Allah to have cancer in its feet – those very feet that help it to stand on the necks of the poor the world over. So what should we do with Adam and Steve? When you go to hospital to meet a cancer
15 patient, do you argue, do you shout? No, you take the person sweet grapes and bright flowers. Gentle persuasion, reciting the words of Allah as revealed in the Koran, will help Adam turn away from Steve and start looking at Eve.

20 *Riaz's sermon[518] above is interrupted by a brick[519] crashing through the window and grazing[520] Tahira's forehead. Hat instinctively guards and comforts Tahira. Riaz is shocked. A stream of rubbish bags and bottles, accompanied[521] by chants of "Paki go home", follows. Chad rushes out, brandishing a cleaver, followed by Shahid. A Young Man with two oth-
25 ers can be seen with bricks in their hands. The two racists scarper[522] at the sight of Chad, while the Young Man is momentarily too stunned[523] to move. Chad floors[524] him and is about to hack[525] at him with the cleaver when he is stopped by Shahid.*

Shahid (*to Chad*) No, Chad! No!

---

512 to unfurl: to unroll
513 awkwardly: in a way showing you are uncomfortable or embarrassed
514 azaan: Muslim call to prayer that summarises Islamic belief
515 fanned: spread out
516 Adam and Steve: i.e, a homosexual relationship
517 to reveal: to show openly what was not known before
518 sermon: talk on a religious subject
519 brick: *Ziegelstein*
520 to graze: to touch lightly while passing
521 accompanied by: happening at the same time
522 to scarper (colloquial, BE): to run away
523 stunned: surprised and shocked
524 to floor: to make s.o. fall down
525 to hack: to cut with heavy blows

Young Man (*spits at them*) Paki! Paki! Paki!

Shahid (*to the Young Man*) What the fuck has this family ever done to you? Have they come to your house? Abused[526] you? Thrown stones? Did they make you live in these stinking flats?

Young Man (*grows more venomous*[527]) Paki! Paki! Paki! You stolen our   5
jobs! Taken our housing! Paki got everything! Give it back and go back home!

Chad Come here again and I'll hack your head off in the halal[528] way!

He swings his cleaver down powerfully and the Young Man scarpers.
(*To Shahid.*) Thanks, brother. If you hadn't held me back, I might have   10
done something powerful, you know.

Riaz comes up behind the boys, with Tahira, Hat, Brownlow in tow.

Riaz It takes courage to hold back. In the fierce heat of battle, you kept your head, Shahid. The true mark of a leader.

Chad He a lion – my lion!   15

Riaz (*complimenting Shahid*) Sher-e-Khan[529]! Come, come, we must eat to mark the occasion!

Chad (*to Riaz*) Shahid's ammi sent some pakoras, brother.

Riaz What better at this moment of triumph!

Chad (*offering Shahid's pakoras*) Right tasty, these aubergine pakoras.   20

Riaz (*taking a pakora*) Nothing ever compares with mother's cooking, eh, Shahid?

Shahid She used to make them for Papa.

Chad (*handing Shahid a plastic bag*) For you.

Shahid What is it?   25

Chad Look.

Shahid (*extracting a white cotton salwar kameez*[530]) It's beautiful.

Chad Yeah!

Shahid For me?

Chad Course. Put it on.   30

Shahid Now?

Riaz Yes, yes, come, Shahid – Tahira will turn her back while we help you change.

---

[526] to abuse: to mistreat
[527] venomous: hateful
[528] halal (Arabic): in the manner of Islamic law when slaughtering animals for food
[529] Sher-e-khan (Hindi/Urdu): tiger king
[530] salwar kameez: loose-fitting shirt and trousers worn by men and women in southeast Asia

Shahid changes, helped by the others. Chad fits a white kufie (Muslim prayer cap) on him as the final act.

Hat Brother, you look magnificent!

Shahid Thanks, Hat.

5 **Chad** How d'you feel?

Shahid A little strange.

Chad Strange?

Shahid But good, good.

Chad What do you think, brother Riaz?

10 **Riaz** (*complimenting*) Now our Shahid Hasan looks a proper Muslim saint! Do you see, Tahira?

Tahira demurely[531] offers Shahid the pakoras.

Tahira May our very own Sher-e-Khan continue to show wisdom and strength!

15 **Riaz** Have some, to mark the occasion, from the hands of your own sister.

Shahid After you.

Hat takes a pakora from Tahira, followed by Riaz.

Hat These pakoras are better than my dad's! (*To Tahira.*) Hey, you think

20 they like spinach for Popeye[532]?

Chad You a fool, yaar, if you think saag[533] will give you strength like Shahid's!

Tahira That inborn, cos[534] he is a Hasan[535], like the Blessed[536] Martyr's son!

25 *Riaz looks at Tahira, then at the pakora.*

Riaz (*to Shahid*) Your ammi made these?

Shahid Yes.

Riaz Are you sure?

Shahid The only thing Zulma ever cooked was Chili's ... you know

30 what.

---

[531] demurely [dɪˈmjʊəli]: quietly, modestly, in a reserved manner

[532] Popeye: comic figure who increases his strength by eating spinach [ˈspɪnɪdʒ]

[533] saag (Hindi): a dish with spinach

[534] cos (colloquial): because

[535] Hasan: Al-Hasan ibn (625 AD – 669 AD): an important figure in Islam, the son of Fatimah, the daughter of the Islamic prophet Muhammad – She is said to have died of injuries acquired while defending her husband.

[536] blessed [ˈblesɪd]: *gesegnet*

Riaz (*expansive*[537]) *Mash-a-Allah*[538]! This is a miracle. The mother of Shahid Hasan is blessed! Chad, look, look at this.

He holds out the pakora on his palm[539] *for Chad and the others to consider*[540].

Chad What am I looking at, brother? I mean – it's a very well-made pakora. 5

Riaz Can't you see – there, running along the length of the pakora – from right to left. Tahira – can you see it?

Tahira Yes! I can make something out – dark – coming through the batter[541]. 10

Riaz It is *aliph*[542] – the first letter of the holy language in which our blessed Koran is written. We have been granted a sign! Through Shahid here.

Shahid What sign, Riaz?

Riaz (*urgent*[543]) Dr Brownlow – we have a miracle in our hands! Allah 15 has sent a message.

Shahid Is the message to carry on the vigil?

Riaz The racists all know now what to expect if they continue to abuse our friend.

Shahid They might return with greater force. 20

Riaz Then we shall be ready for them, *insha'Allah*[544]. But news of this miracle will bring many more people to our side for the great work yet to come. The Iranians will hear of this. And then all will see how we stand strong when the wrathful[545] sword of Allah slices through the air of injustice Mussulmans[546] breathe everyday in this country. 25

Shahid I have to go – family business …

Riaz (*expansive*) Of course, of course. Take Tahira with you. We will make all preparations to unveil[547] this miracle before the unbelieving world. Chad, inform Moulana Darapuria we must meet urgently[548].

---

[537] expansive: with high spirits, extravagant
[538] Mash-a-Allah (Arabic): God has willed it.
[539] palm: the inner surface of the hand without the fingers
[540] to consider: (here): to look carefully at s.th.
[541] batter: *Backteig*
[542] aliph: first letter in Arabic
[543] urgent: showing you think s.th. needs to be dealt with immediately
[544] insha' Alla (Arabic): God willing
[545] wrathful: full of great anger
[546] Mussulman (old-fashioned): Muslim
[547] to unveil: to reveal, to show what has been hidden
[548] urgently: as soon as possible because it's important

Shahid puts his jacket on and rushes out. Tahira follows him out. Strapper is lounging by the door.

Tahira Where are we going?

Shahid Personal business – family, you know. I'll be back soon.

5 **Tahira** But you mustn't be alone at this time.

Shahid I will be all right.

Tahira I'm really not afraid.

Shahid But I'd be afraid for you.

Tahira (*simpering*[549]) You are a true Hasan!

10 *Shahid ushers her back in and walks off, followed by Strapper.*

Strapper I could fix you up[550], you know.

Shahid I'm not buying anything from you.

Strapper Why not? I fixed you up at the rave, didn't I? Weren't my shit[551] the best you had? Straight up[552], we got suppliers that don't do

15 dirty[553].

Shahid Listen, I got no charity, okay?

Strapper *Zakat*[554].

Shahid What?

Strapper That's what them Muslim brothers call it, giving charity to the

20 needy.

Shahid You don't look needy to me and I'm not in the giving mood.

Strapper Stop running from your own – they's the only ones to depend on, when the shit hits the fan[555].

Shahid I'm not running from anyone. Except you.

25 **Strapper** No need to insult, Paki.

Shahid I'm not a Paki!

Strapper Course you are. We all are, those who've been left behind.

Strapper runs off, as Shahid heads to Deedee's. Music, as he rushes through a wintry London night.

---

[549] to simper: to smile in a silly way

[550] to fix s.o. up (slang): to supply with drugs

[551] shit (slang): cannabis or heroin

[552] straight up (slang): pure

[553] to do dirty (slang): to reduce the quality of drugs by adding other non-drug substances

[554] zakat (Arabic): an annual tax that Muslims pay to help the needy in the community

[555] when the shit hits the fan (colloquial): when s.o. in authority finds out that s.o. has done s.th. wrong

Deedee's house. Deedee has prepared a candlelit dinner. Shahid rushes in.

Shahid Sorry, sorry, sorry.
Beat, as Deedee looks at how Shahid is dressed.   5
Deedee In your pyjamas already?
Shahid You don't know what's happening out there – urgent brother business! Chad was this close to carving some serious meat.[556]
Deedee No surprise there – he wanted to chuck[557] a bomb on his parents. That's after he met Riaz, of course. Changed his name from Trevor 10
Buss to Muhammad Shahabuddin Ali-Shah.
Shahid What? Chad?
Deedee He was brought up by white foster parents[558]. Foul-mouthed[559] and racist to everyone but their son. No wonder he became a shooter[560]. Riaz took him under his wing[561]. Insisted everyone call him by 15
his whole new name, even when playing football. His mates got fed up shouting, "Pass the ball, Muhammad Shahabuddin Ali-Shah – on my head, Muhammad Shahabuddin Ali-Shah." So he became Chad.
She offers some wine. Shahid makes a face.
Are there any pleasures you don't eschew[562]? Or is it only salted las- 20
si[563] you drink?
Shahid What about fighting racism?
Deedee Is that what you think Riaz does?
Shahid He is pure of purpose and risking his life guarding the flat of a persecuted couple right now.   25
Deedee Riaz denounced his own father for drinking alcohol and praying in his armchair and not on his knees. He made you wear that, didn't he?
Shahid What's wrong with them?

---

[556] Chad was this close to carving (to carve: to cut a large piece of cooked meat into smaller pieces for eating) serious meat. (colloquial): Chad was close to injuring or killing s.o. with a knife.
[557] to chuck (colloquial, BE): to throw
[558] foster parents: a couple that brings up a child without becoming the legal parents
[559] foul-mouthed: using offensive, obscene language
[560] shooter: a person who takes drugs by injection *(Spritze)*
[561] to take s.o. under your wing: to take care of and help s.o.
[562] to eschew [ɪsˈtʃuː] (formal): to deliberately avoid
[563] lassi [ˈlæsi] (Hindi): a cool south Asian drink made from yogurt or buttermilk

Deedee Didn't take you for a disciple[564].

Shahid Can't I admire him for his courage?

The doorbell rings. Deedee opens the door to Chili.

Chili What are you called when someone's asking?

5 **Deedee** Deedee. Deedee Osgood.

Chili (*kissing her hands*) Tell me, Deedee Osgood, is my baby bro safe in your hands?

Deedee (*appraising him*) You must be Chili.

Chili At your service.

10 **Deedee** One Hasan at a time is more than enough.

Chili Are you sure?

Deedee laughs.

A woman's laugh – better than any rush[565] known to man.

Deedee Quite the priest. I can't imagine you giving a sermon.

15 **Chili** I could be a very Jesus in bed.

Shahid What you doing here, Chili?

Chili I was concerned, bro. Thought that bad posse might have messed with[566] you.

Deedee They have.

20 **Chili** (*to Shahid*) Just say the word, and Chili will have a friendly chat.

Shahid I'll take care of myself.

Chili Just take her in your arms. Want me to demonstrate?

Deedee I'm not clean enough for him. I've become a sort of pork chop[567].

Chili But his knees used to go weak at the sight of a bacon sarnie[568]. (*to*

25 *Shahid*) If Papa were alive, he'd have a fucking heart attack seeing you dressed like Ali Baba[569].

Shahid That's who we are, bro! (*to Deedee*) We don't sit swigging[570] wine all evening!

Deedee What alternative are you offering?

30 **Chili** And you two not even married yet …!

---

[564] disciple [dɪˈsaɪpl]: a person who believes in and follows the teachings of a religious or political leader

[565] rush: sudden feeling of excitement or pleasure, often produced by drugs

[566] to mess with s.o.: to get involved with s.o. that may result in violence

[567] pork chop: *Schweinekotelett* (a reference to the fact that pork is taboo for Muslims)

[568] sarnie (colloquial, BE): sandwich

[569] Ali Baba: fictional character from medieval Arabic literature, the hero in the adventure tale of *Ali Baba and the Forty Thieves*

[570] to swig (colloquial): to take a quick drink of s.th.

He picks up a beer and leaves. Pause.

Deedee It's very original, the way you weave[571] Scheherazade[572] into your story. *The Arabian Nights* in Sevenoaks. No one's written like this about England – you have a voice and a future, Shahid.

Shahid is speechless. 5

This is the new literature – when stories from elsewhere slice into[573] conventional England. Rushdie showed there's a gap[574] in modern writing that can only be filled by stories like yours. You could be the real deal[575]. You could be published by Faber and Faber[576] and go to literary parties, accompanied by me. 10

Shahid Yeah?

Deedee If you don't get distracted[577].

Shahid You look ravishing[578], you do.

Deedee Thank you.

Shahid Deedee … 15

She slips his kurta[579] off and sits him on her sofa. Puts on some music and starts applying[580] make-up to turn him androgynous[581], à la Prince. She talks as she works.

Deedee London was full of Arabs in the seventies. They thought they liked girls. Didn't treat us badly but wouldn't talk. So we'd sit in 20 their apartments all night, snorting coke and waiting to be pointed at … Happiest day was being accepted for university. My old man said someone common[582] like me didn't deserve an education … Met

---

[571] to weave: *einflechten*

[572] Scheherazade [ʃəˌherəˈzɑːdə]: legendary Persian queen and the storyteller in *The Arabian Nights: Tales from One Thousand and One Nights*

[573] to slice into: to move into s.th. like a knife

[574] gap: *Lücke* – Indeed Sir Salman Rushdie has written numerous articles about writers from former British colonies making a great impact on traditional British literature.

[575] the real deal: an authentic voice that is successful

[576] Faber and Faber: an established publishing house that now belongs to Macmillan – It is Hanif Kureishi's publisher.

[577] to distract: to divert, to take your attention away from what you are doing

[578] ravishing: delightful, lovely

[579] kurta (Hindi, Urdu): loose-fitting shirt that reaches to the knees, worn in India, Pakistan, Afghanistan, Bangladesh, Nepal, and Sri Lanka

[580] to apply: to put or spread on a surface

[581] androgynous [ænˈdrɒdʒənəs]: having both female and male characteristics

[582] common: *gewöhnlich*

Brownlow there. Off to picket lines[583], demonstrations and Greenham Common[584] – activists together … When I think about how far I've come, I'm proud of what I've done.

Shahid Why are you sad, then?

5 **Deedee** Am I?

Shahid A little.

Deedee The price might have been too high … I gave up the possibility of children for what?

She invites him to parade.

10 **Shahid** Now?

Deedee There's only now. Let's see how well you know your Prince.

He parades to music from Prince's Black Album.

Shahid (*with a flourish*[585], *quoting Prince's songs*) Aw[586]! Lovesexy[587]! Baby I'm a Star[588]!

15 **Deedee** Still like Prince? Your friend Chad?

Shahid U Got that Look[589] …! Nah[590] – he's[591] Rockhard in a Funky Place[592].

Deedee (*joining in the game*) I knew him with a Raspberry Beret[593]on his head.

20 **Shahid** (*concerned*[594]) Condition of the Heart[595]?

---

[583] picket line: group of people standing in front of the entrance of a building or around it to prevent people from entering either in a political protest or because of a strike

[584] Greenham Common: formerly a military airfield in Berkshire, England – From 1981 until 2000 "women's peace camps" were established in protest at the deployment of the cruise missiles.

[585] with a flourish: with an exaggerated movement

[586] aw [ɔː]: expression of approval

[587] Lovesexy: Prince album released in 1988

[588] Baby I'm a Star: song written and recorded by Prince from his album *Purple Rain* in 1984

[589] U Got The Look: Prince song released in a 1987

[590] nah (slang): no

[591] he: a reference to Chad

[592] Rockhard in a Funky Place: song on *The Black Album* (1987)

[593] Raspberry Beret: song by Prince and The Revolution. It was a single from their 1985 album, *Around the World in a Day.*

[594] concerned: worried

[595] Condition of the Heart: song in *Around the World in a Day*

Deedee No. Sign o' the Times[596]. Purple Rain[597]. He was a One Man Jam[598]!

Shahid Hot Thing[599]! That's action to the max[600]. Like when you were on picket lines.

Deedee Our cause was clearer then. We questioned. All authority. Religion.

Shahid (*jibing*[601]) Now you teach post-colonial literature[602].

Deedee Thatcher[603]'s worn everyone down[604]. (*Defiant*[605].) So let's just Dance to the Music of the World[606]!

Shahid You Can Be My Teacher[607], driving a Little Red Corvette[608]!

Deedee I Wanna Be your Lover[609]!

Shahid Let's do Le Grind[610]!

Deedee Let's Go Crazy[611]!

They dance.

Shahid Can't stay tonight.

She stops.

Deedee Why?

Shahid Brother action, you know.

Deedee No, I don't.

Beat.

---

[596] Sign o' the Times: album and song by Prince (1987)

[597] Purple Rain: song and album by Prince (1984)

[598] One Man Jam: early song by Prince before he was a star (1970s) – jam: difficult situation

[599] Hot Thing: song on *Sign o' the Times* (1987)

[600] max: maximum

[601] to jibe: to say s.th. with the intention of making s.o. look silly or to embarrass this person

[602] post-colonial literature: literature written by writers from the former colonies of the British Empire

[603] Thatcher: Margaret Thatcher, British Prime Minister (1979–1990), known for her pro-business, anti-union policy

[604] to wear, wore, worn s.o. down: to make s.o. weaker or less determined by continuously attacking or putting pressure on this person

[605] defiant: refusing to obey, opposed to authority

[606] Dance to the Music of the World: song on the 1977 album *Minneapolis Genius, 94 East*

[607] You Can Be My Teacher: song on the album, *Prince With 94 East's You Can Be My Teacher* (1970s)

[608] Little Red Corvette: song released on the album *1999* in 1982

[609] I Wanna Be Your Lover: song released on the album, *Prince* in 1979

[610] Le Grind: song on *The Black Album* (1987)

[611] Let's Go Crazy: song on the album, *Purple Rain* (1984)

Shahid Riaz has seen a miracle[612].

Deedee Fuck[613]!

Shahid Can't you just make me come[614]?

Beat.

5 **Deedee** You know what you want – that's something at least. Would your friends say you're a hypocrite[615], coming here for a fuck after God's shown Riaz a miracle?

Shahid I do want to be with you.

Deedee There's quicker ways to get relief[616].

10 **Shahid** Don't put me off[617], Deedee.

Deedee Why not? Do you really understand what's going on with Riaz?

Shahid Please, Deedee …

Deedee You want me – fine. What're you going to do for me?

15 **Shahid** What do you want me to do?

Deedee Thinking for yourself will be a start. He's using you for his own ends.

Shahid Aren't you?

Deedee You came to me with your writing, remember? Do you want
20 Riaz to destroy your creativity?

Shahid Why do you assume he'll do that? He's given me his poems to work on.

Deedee I don't trust him.

Shahid You don't like him.

25 **Deedee** He's dangerous.

Shahid He needs me – I'm going back.

He picks up his jacket and exits.

Deedee (*shouting after him*) You've got to decide, Shahid – who really are your people?

30 *Interval[618].*

---

[612] miracle: *Wunder*

[613] Fuck!: *Scheiße!*

[614] to come: (here) to have an orgasm

[615] hypocrite ['hɪpəkrɪt]: *Heuchler*

[616] relief: (here): a reduction of sexual tension

[617] to put s.o. off: (here): to confuse, to upset, to frustrate

[618] interval: short break

Act Two

Scene Ten

Shahid's digs. Morning. Shahid is working at his desk. Chad enters, with Hat.

Chad Hey, Shahid, brother Riaz had the delectation[1] of meeting your brother in the hallway[2] earlier. An' you know what happened? There was an incident. 5

Shahid What incident?

Hat Chili threatened brother Riaz.

Shahid Sorry?

Hat He claimed the brother wearing one of his shirts. 10

Shahid Oh, no.

Hat Riaz didn't know what he was talking about.

Shahid (*to Chad*) Did you tell Riaz?

Chad (*pointedly*[3]) It ain't[4] him nuisancing[5] me right now.

Shahid Who do you mean? 15

Chad You holding something back, Shahid?

Shahid Listen, Chad – you know, brother, the first time we met, an' I told you that as a Paki, I went through a lot of shit[6]? I wanted to say to you, Trev –

Chad Did you call me Trev? 20

Shahid Yeah, I was trying to say –

Chad No more Trev. Me a Muslim. Like Mohammed Ali[7]. We don't apologise for ourselves. We are people who say one important thing – that pleasure and self-absorption[8] isn't everything.

Hat Riaz says it is a bottomless basket. 25

Chad Ain't that a wicked[9] phrase[10]? One pleasure – unless there are strong limits – can only lead to another. Until we become beasts. The people paint their faces.

---

[1] delectation (formal, humorous): pleasure
[2] hallway: *Flur*
[3] pointedly: in a way intending to show criticism
[4] ain't (slang): isn't
[5] to nuisance (colloquial): to annoy, to irritate
[6] shit (slang): hard times
[7] Mohammed Ali (originally Cassius Marcellus Clay, Jr) (1942–): American professional boxer who converted to Islam in 1975
[8] self-absorption: only being concerned about yourself
[9] wicked ['wɪkɪd]: (here): clever, cool
[10] phrase: expression

Shahid What?

Chad They wear aftershave. And they paint their faces. What happened to the clothes I gave you?

Shahid I was too cold.

5 **Chad** You hear the Iranians planning to put the *fatwa* on the writer?

Shahid What's a *fatwa*?

Chad That when Allah take a cleaver against a sinner[11] – like what I did against that racist.

Hat Only it green.

10 **Chad** What?

Hat Allah is green, so his sword is green – you know, the colour of fertile[12] land.

Chad Yeah, Allah the first environmentalist. Anyway, it the law, once it passed by the Iranians. It legal then to take action against the blas-
15 phemer. And now there's been a confirmation[13], no one can doubt it. It will force Iranians to issue[14] the *fatwa*.

Hat What confirmation?

Chad (*stating the obvious*) We have been given a miraculous sign.

Hat We blessed! What sort of sign?

20 **Chad** An arrow.

Shahid An arrow?

Chad Yeah, it's an arrow pointing straight at the author.

Hat What type of arrow?

Chad I'll clip[15] you upside[16] your head! How many bloody[17] type of ar-
25 rows are there? You idiot. I'll just say this. It's an arrow in an egg-plant.

Hat How can you plant an egg?

Chad You fool, Hat, don't problem up a brother! Moulana Darapuria has now given his confirmation that the aubergine[18] wrapped in Shahid's
30 pakora is a divine[19] symbol. And we're exhibiting the righteous[20]

---

[11] sinner: *Sünder, -in*
[12] fertile ['fɜːtaɪl]: having the quality of being very good for growing plants
[13] confirmation: a document or piece of evidence that shows that s.th. is true
[14] to issue: to announce formally
[15] to clip: to cut
[16] upside (unusual English): with the top at the bottom
[17] bloody (colloquial, BE): *verdammt*
[18] aubergine: eggplant
[19] divine: connected with God
[20] righteous: morally good and right

78

aubergine right here! Riaz wants a squad[21] of us brothers to watch the door, make sure the crowds behave, and the press don't turn hot lights on God's message.

Tahira enters with the aubergine on a silver salver[22]. She places it in the middle of the room and begins circumambulating[23], followed by streams of others.   5

Tahira God has granted[24] me the sight. Thanks to Shahid.

Hat It's true, Shahid! You can see the arrow!

Chad Pointing straight at Islington[25].

Shahid How do you know it's Islington?   10

Chad It where the writer live.

Shahid My room's going to be wrecked[26] by all these people.

Riaz enters, as the "pilgrims[27]" begin chanting.

Riaz *As-salaam a-leikum[28]*, Shahid. You see how far-reaching is the power of Allah.   15

Shahid I didn't realise Allah was vegetarian.

Riaz clocks[29] Shahid momentarily, then laughs.

Riaz You have a good way with your words. (*Taking Shahid aside.*) Our people, most of them are from villages, half-literate[30] and not wanted here. These miracles give them a voice in this land of so-called free   20
expression. We who are educated, it is our duty to give this miracle a shape. I understand the Ayatollah is getting ready to make a big announcement.

Shahid Do you know what the *fatwa* will say?

Riaz It is a call to all Muslims to defend the faith against blasphemers.   25

Shahid What does that mean?

Riaz Surely it is obvious. The *fatwa* requires us to take whatever action is necessary. Just like the action we took against the racists. That writer insults us. To be against racism is to also be against blasphemers. I can see this troubles you, Shahid. Let us discuss this openly, like   30

---

[21] squad: small group
[22] salver: large, metal plate
[23] to circumambulate (formal, humorous): to walk around
[24] to grant: to give in a formal manner
[25] Islington: inner-city district of London
[26] to wreck: to damage
[27] pilgrim: *Pilger*
[28] As-salaam a-leikum (Arabic): Peace be upon you.
[29] to clock (slang, BE): to observe, to look at, to notice
[30] half-literate: with little education

a family. I will tell all the brothers to assemble in your room early in the morning.

Brownlow enters, eager to talk to Riaz, who draws[31] Shahid further away.

5   How is the typing coming?

Shahid I've had to change a few things in your poems.

Riaz Excellent. Are you having to translate my work into current[32] English?

Shahid No, it's more like –

10 **Riaz** Smoothing out[33]?

Shahid Yes.

Riaz Good. What did you think of my poem?

Shahid Which one?

Riaz "The Wrath." "The Wrath."

15 **Shahid** I – uh[34] – haven't got to that one yet.

Riaz Chad says you have had some work published.

Shahid In a magazine. A while ago.

Riaz What was it called?

Shahid "Paki Wog[35] Fuck Off[36] Home."

20 **Riaz** Did they publish it?

Shahid They were going to. Except my ammi tore up the manuscript. Said no one would want to read such filth[37].

Riaz Muslims like us will never get accepted.

Shahid Oh no, there's nothing more fashionable than people like us.

25   You, brother, could have a wide appeal if the media knew of you.

Riaz The media, yes. You must submit[38] an article on this matter of blasphemy to the national newspapers.

Shahid It's difficult, with my room now a pilgrimage site[39] ...

Riaz How are you getting on with Tahira?

30 **Shahid** Fine, fine. She's a good brother – (*correcting himself*) sister.

---

[31] to draw: to move by pulling gently
[32] current: modern, of the present time
[33] to smooth out: to remove mistakes and make stylistically better
[34] uh [ʌ]: sound made when you are not sure what to say next
[35] wog (slang, BE): offensive expression for s.o. who has dark skin
[36] fuck off (slang): go
[37] filth (fig.): dirt
[38] to submit: to hand in
[39] pilgrimage site: a place pilgrims go to

Riaz An example to all our women. Modest. Obedient[40]. She will make a good companion to a true young Muslim leader. And she wears no make-up.

Shahid What?

Riaz (*reassuring*[41]) Let me see what I can do about your room. (*Turning to Brownlow.*) Welcome, Dr Brownlow to the site of the bona-fide[42] miracle.

Brownlow I have arranged for Councillor[43] R-R-Rudder to attend.

Riaz Excellent, excellent. You see, Shahid, all the great powers in the community are gathering in support of our cause. Councillor George Rugman Rudder is Labour leader of the entire elected council here. Will you write down what he says? (*To Brownlow.*) We need him to deliver[44] a bigger place, Dr Brownlow.

Councillor Rudder enters, sporting[45] *a huge cigar. The crowd gathers behind Riaz and Brownlow, to welcome Rudder.*

Rudder Hello there, people! Hello, all!

Riaz, Brownlow and Rudder shake hands while Hat takes a photo, and Shahid scribbles[46] *furiously*[47].

Riaz Thank you for coming, Mr Rudder. We knew you would pay your respects[48].

Rudder Naturally, naturally. What a marvellous crowd, worshipping[49] the fruit of the earth! What a popular aubergine, top of the vegetable table[50]! What a sound[51] method of communication the miracle is! Thank God a Tory[52] borough[53] wasn't chosen!

Riaz Mr Rudder, our sincere[54] thanks again for letting us use a private house in this public way. We understand how illegal it normally is.

---

[40] obedient: doing as you are told
[41] to reassure: to say s.th. to s.o. that will make this person less worried
[42] bona-fide (Latin): genuine, real
[43] councillor: member of the town council (*Gemeinderat*)
[44] to deliver: to arrange for, to provide
[45] to sport: to have in a proud way
[46] to scribble: to write quickly and carelessly
[47] furiously: with great speed without thought about making mistakes
[48] to pay your respects: to show your respect for s.th. or s.o. by coming to visit
[49] to worship: to love and admire s.th. very much, to show great respect for s.o. or s.th.
[50] vegetable table: list of vegetables considered healthy
[51] sound: sensible, good
[52] Tory (colloquial, BE): having to do with the British Conservative Party
[53] borough['bʌrə]: local government, district
[54] sincere: *aufrichtig*

The whole community is eternally[55] grateful. You are a true friend of Asia.

Chad (*while continuing to circle the aubergine*) Friend of Asia!

Hat (*picking up the chant*) And of Southall[56]!

5 **Tahira** And of Newham[57]!

Chad And of Brick Lane[58] – Asia's best friend!

Hat and Tahira lead in the chant "Friend of Asia, friend of Asia, Asia's best friend!" as they continue to circle the aubergine.

Rudder Yes, and I'll be rewarded in heaven, no doubt. The Seventh Day
10 Adventists[59] have expressed deep satisfaction, and, it is said, mention my ailments[60] in their prayers. Rastafarians[61] shake my hand as I walk my dog. I am East London's one true Anglo-Saxon friend! (*To Riaz and Brownlow.*) Naturally, I have been generous enough to use my influence, against very racialist opposition, to open a private house in
15 this way. But you are also smart enough to know, Riaz – and you are a smarty – that it can't last for ever.

Riaz Which is why, Councillor Rudder, we have been thinking so much about the Town Hall for the preservation[62] of the sacred miracle in public.

20 **Brownlow** (*taken aback*[63]) Y-y-yes, the T-T-Town Hall.

Rudder The Town Hall?

Riaz Is there a reason why not?

Chad (*while continuing to circle the aubergine*) Rudder, Rudder, Rudder – he's our Asian brother!

25 *Crowd picks up*[64] *the chant.*

---

55 eternally: for all times
56 Southall: suburban district of west London with a large South Asian population
57 Newham: district in east London with 38% of the population being Asian
58 Brick Lane: street in the London Borough of Tower Hamlets, in the East End of London – It has a large Bangladeshi population.
59 Seventh Day Adventists: conservative Christian denomination founded in America in 1863, which observes the Sabbath on Saturday, places emphasis on good health, and believes the second coming of Jesus Christ is to take place soon
60 ailment ['eɪlmənt]: illness that is not serious
61 Rastafarian: a person who believes in Rastafarianism, a monotheistic, religious movement that arose in a Christian culture in Jamaica in the 1930s. They worship Haile Selassie I of Ethiopia, former Emperor of Ethiopia (1930–1936 and 1941–1974), as a God. Cannabis is sometimes used in religious ceremonies and western culture is rejected. Black nationalism also plays a role.
62 preservation: the act of making sure s.th. stays in its original condition
63 taken aback: very shocked and surprised
64 to pick up: to join in with s.th. and continue with it

Rudder Yes, yes, perhaps the Town Hall. There's plenty of room. Most of it between the ears of the people who work there.

Riaz It will have to be in the foyer[65]. There is already hanging there a picture of Nelson Mandela[66]. We must not be ghettoised[67].

Chad No! No! No! Ghettoisation – no! 5

Crowd picks up the chant.

Rudder Let me first witness[68] this phenomenal example of God's signature.

They part[69] to allow him to enter.

(*Aside, to Brownlow.*) Of course, revelations[70] are faith's[71] aberra- 10 tion[72], an amusement at the most. But whatever helps the Labour Party get re-elected mustn't be scoffed at[73]. Let's hope they curry this blue fruit. Brinjal[74], I believe it's called. I could murder an Indian[75], couldn't you?

He proceeds[76] to a viewing of the Miraculous Aubergine. Music. All dis- 15 perse[77].

Shahid returns to his computer. Night.

Deedee enters, carrying her bag of books and notes.

Shahid (*excited*) I wasn't sure you'd come, Deedee.

She sees "the miracle" on the salver. 20

Deedee (*laughing*) God in a pulpy[78] vegetable!

Shahid Is Prince culture? Or just what you think we darkies[79] understand?

---

[65] foyer ['fɔɪeɪ]: a large, open space inside the entrance of a theatre, official building, or hotel where people can meet or wait

[66] Nelson Mandela (1918–): President of South Africa from 1994 to 1999, and the first South African president to be elected in a fully representative democratic election. Before his presidency, Mandela was an anti-apartheid activist who spent 27 years in prison.

[67] to ghettoise: to force to live in a ghetto

[68] to witness: to see, to be present at, to get to know first hand

[69] to part: to move from side to side to allow s.o. to pass

[70] revelation: s.th. revealed in a surprising, dramatic way

[71] faith: religion

[72] aberration: act that is not normal, usual, or expected

[73] to scoff at: to mock, to not consider to be serious

[74] Brinjal (Arabic): aubergine

[75] I could murder an Indian …: Rudder is making political use of the hatred Pakistanis feel for Indians.

[76] to proceed: to do s.th. next, after having done s.th. else

[77] to disperse: to go away in many different directions

[78] pulpy: soft and wet

[79] darky (negative, slang): a person with dark skin

Deedee I'm prepared to include voodoo[80] as a subject of study because it's part of the culture of some Caribbean Blacks, but that doesn't mean I have to believe in it.

Shahid Please, Deedee. I've got to make up my own mind about things!
5 I don't always want to be on the outside.

Deedee Don't ask me to believe in a communicating vegetable – and nor am I going to compete with one either. I'd heard books were on the way out, so now Riaz will want libraries to be replaced by greengrocers.

10 **Shahid** It doesn't matter any more! The Iranians are involved[81]. They want to ban the book! I need help, Deedee.

Deedee starts laughing.

What is it? Deedee?!

Deedee Give me your aubergine[82]. Stick it in my earth[83] and let me bless
15 it with my holy waters[84].

Shahid I've forced Riaz into an open debate tomorrow.

Deedee What are you going to say?

Shahid Give me a precis[85]? I haven't got time to become educated first.

He gathers[86] his notebook and stands ready.

20 **Deedee** Right then. There's nothing new in wanting to ban a book. We've been down this road before – with Joyce[87], Lawrence[88], Miller[89], Nabokov[90]. They were all censored in their time. And what did it change? People still read the banned books. Censorship's never been

---

[80] voodoo ['vu:du:]: a religion in Haiti in which magic plays a central role
[81] involved: taking part in, connected with
[82] aubergine (fig.): penis
[83] earth (fig.): vagina
[84] holy waters (fig.): secretion that occurs with an orgasm
[85] precis ['preɪsiː]: a summary of a piece of writing or a speech with the main points
[86] to gather: (here): to take into your hands
[87] James Joyce (1882–1941): Irish novelist and poet –His novel, **Ulysses** (1922) was censored in the USA for obscenity.
[88] D. H. Lawrence (1885–1930): English novelist, poet – His novel, **Lady Chatterley's Lover** was censored or banned in its complete version in the United States and Great Britain until the 1960s as pornography.
[89] Henry Miller (1891–1980): American novelist and painter, many of whose novels were banned in the United States until the 1960s because of their explicit sexual content
[90] Vladimir Vladimirovich Nabokov (1899–1977): Russian-American novelist and short story writer – His novel, **Lolita** (1955) was banned for a time in Great Britain and France because it contained a love affair between a 12-year-old girl and an older man.

successful. The last time it was tried was during the Inquisition[91] –
and that led to the fall of the very Church it was trying to protect. Not
what your friends really want, is it?

Shahid (*impressed*) Can you take them on[92] instead of me?

Deedee And what will you do?   5

Shahid Cook you dinner?

Deedee I'll pass on[93] that. These are your people, remember?

Shahid I get confused sometimes.

She hands him a pile of books from her bag.

Will you stay?   10

Deedee You've got work to do tonight.

Shahid It'll help me focus.

Deedee The miracle and me aren't meant to be in the same room.

She gathers her things and leaves.

Shahid Fuck!   15

Shahid resumes[94] working on his computer, flicking through the books.
Chili enters with Strapper.

What's he doing here?

Chili That's Strapper –

Shahid I know who he is! I'm working, Chili!   20

Chili starts scrabbling about[95] on the floor, hunting for his stash.

Strapper Come on, Chili!

Shahid What the fuck's going on?

Chili Didn't think you'd met my partner.

He finds the stash he's hidden in the copy of **Satanic Verses** *that Deedee* 25
had given Shahid.

Ah, there you are, my beauty!

Strapper Come on, Chili, I'm dying here.

Chili Patience, Strap-boy, there's an art to satiating[96] hunger.

He carefully unwraps the coke, cuts it up on a page and snorts.   30

---

[91] the Inquisition: a body within the Roman Catholic Church that sought to suppress
heretics within the Church, starting in the 12th century – The Spanish Inquisition
was especially virulent in the 15th and 16th centuries. It tortured and burned alive
suspected heretics and many Jewish converts. Written documents that reflected the
new ideas of Protestantism and humanism were frequently censored or banned.

[92] to take s.o. on: to oppose, to fight

[93] to pass on s.th.: (here): to decide not to accept s.o.'s offer

[94] to resume: to continue with s.th. that you had started before

[95] to scrabble about: to try to find s.th. in a hurry and with difficulty by moving your
hands or feet about quickly, without little control

[96] to satiate ['seɪʃieɪt]: to supply to satisfaction

Shahid (*to Chili*) Your closest brush[97] with literature, ever.

Chili (*passing the score[98] to Strapper*) There you go, Strap – you gotta trust me.

Strapper snorts.

5   (*to Shahid*) Got a drink?

Shahid Fortunately not.

Chili Been to evening prayers?

Shahid Go home, Chili. If you can't, just leave me be. I got things to do.

10 *Suddenly, two Heavies[99] burst in. Strapper shrinks back[100] in fear. Shahid is frozen in shock.*

Strapper I told you! Chili!

Heavy 1 (*to Chili*) So?

Chili hands over the money. The man counts it, snorts[101] derisively[102] and
15 *takes a step forward. Chili hands over his keys.*

Heavy 2 He's got brains.

Chili The Beamer parked outside. Full tank, too.

Heavy 1 Pardon?

Chili Full tank.

20 *The Heavies look at each other, and kick Chili repeatedly. They leave. Shahid scrambles[103] over to his brother.*

Shahid What's happening to you, Chili?

Chili pushes him away and goes to the still-whimpering Strapper.

Chili (*knocks on Strapper's head*) There's someone in there. Oh, yes, I
25   know there is.

Strapper Christ. They … they gone?

Chili For now.

Strapper Right. Phew[104].

Chili (*to Shahid, as he lays Strapper down gently*) Floor's very hard.
30   Where's your landlord[105]?

Shahid What's going on, Chili?

---

[97] brush: contact

[98] score: drugs that have been obtained illegally

[99] heavy: large, strong man, working for a gangster, whose job it is to carry out the orders of his boss with violence if necessary

[100] to shrink back: to move back suddenly because of being frightened

[101] to snort: *schnauben*

[102] derisively: in a manner showing you think s.o. is ridiculous, mockingly

[103] to scramble: to move quickly and with difficulty, using your hands to help you

[104] phew [fju:]: an expression of relief *(Erleichterung)*

[105] landlord: the person from whom you rent a house or flat

Chili (*ignoring him*) I want to complain. He's a fucker[106]. (*Beat.*) If Papa were alive, we'd be giving him heart attacks. Which of us, do you think, would he be more horrified by? I'd love to take a picture of you praying on your knees and send it to him in heaven. He'd probably say, "What's my boy doing down there, looking for some money he's dropped?" 5

Shahid, exasperated[107], resumes work on his computer.

There you have it, Strap, my hard-working baby brother. Times are moody[108], I have to admit, but he'll sort us out[109], won't you, bro? Hey, Strap, look at the dreamer. 10

Strapper Like me.

Chili You?

Strapper Yeah, me, man.

Chili They ain't dreams, they're drug hallucinations!

Strapper Fuck off[110], man. You should've sorted the cash[111]! You kept 15 sayin' London was too small a place for ya. Is it small enough for you now, Chili, eh – this small enough?

Chili Shhh, let the boy work, Strap. Hey, what's the score[112], bro?

Shahid (*tetchy[113]*) What's free speech to you, Chili?

Chili Don't bend your knee[114]. 20

Strapper Windbag! You done shat yourself[115] when those heavies came in for their money!

Chili That's just a game, Strap. But this here now –

He clutches hold[116] of Strapper, as he addresses Shahid.

– this here is pure censorship. Nothing terrible will ever happen to us, 25 unless we will it. That's just the way it is. But evil's been done to Strap, practically from day one he's been censored. Don't do this! Stop there! Stay away from that! He don't deserve to be wasted[117]. If you want to fight for anything, fight for him.

---

[106] fucker (slang): *Scheißkerl*
[107] exasperated: very angry and irritated
[108] moody: *launisch*
[109] to sort s.o. out: to find a solution to a person's problem
[110] fuck off (slang): Go to hell!
[111] sorted the cash: made sure the money had been collected
[112] the score: the facts in the present situation
[113] tetchy: bad-tempered, irritable
[114] Don't bend your knee. (colloquial): Don't get overly excited.
[115] done shat (past participle of "to shit") yourself (slang): you were extremely frightened
[116] to clutch hold: to hold s.th. or s.o. tightly
[117] wasted: (here): killed

Shahid I think I want to be a writer.

Chili What's wrong with being a travel agent?

Shahid You try it! Papa left everything to you. Ammi needs you.

Chili You want me to be like all the other Pakis in their dirty shops, hu-
5   mourlessly keeping their eyes only on the pennies dropping in their
palms? Go and work there if you like it so much. I give you my place!
But you won't either. We ain't ones to make sacrifices[118], are we, bro?

Shahid Just go home, Chili, please. Papa worked his arse off[119].

Chili remains silent.

10 (*insistent*[120]) To give us a decent life.

Chili And what is that? Do you know?

He grabs hold of Shahid.

Why won't you tell me?

Shahid Let go of me!

15 **Chili** No one knows!

He slaps[121] Shahid. Shahid goes to punch him, but Chili slaps him again.
Now shut it[122]!

Shahid Fuck, fuck!

Shahid returns to his computer, as Chili and Strapper lie wasted[123].

20 *After a time, Shahid covers his trembling brother with a blanket and
continues working.*

Morning dawns[124]. Chili gets up and takes Strapper out with him.

*There is a knock on the door. Shahid shuts down his computer, tidies him-
self[125] and opens the door to Riaz, Brownlow, Chad and Hat.*

25 **Riaz** *Salaam a-leikum,* Shahid.

Shahid *Wa-leikum salaam*[126].

Riaz and the others take their seats in the room.

Riaz Come, remind everyone of the topic you want to debate.

Chad You call us here for what, when the issue is obvious?

---

[118] sacrifice: *Opfer*

[119] to work your arse off (slang): to work very hard

[120] insistent: demanding s.th. firmly and refusing to accept any opposition

[121] to slap: to hit with the flat part of your hand

[122] it: your mouth

[123] wasted (slang): (here): strongly affected by drugs

[124] to dawn: to begin to grow light

[125] to tidy yourself: to make yourself look neat and tidy again

[126] Wa-leikum salaam (Arabic): May God grant you peace, mercy, and His blessing.

Shahid I hope it is. John Milton[127] said long ago that he who destroys a good book kills reason itself. The best way to respond to the book is to guard against that.

Hat Are you talking of that book?

Shahid Yes, Hat. There's been a long history of books being banned – 5 Joyce's **Ulysses** was burned in New York[128] and then Lawrence, when he wrote **Lady Chatterley's** –

Hat Is that Lawrence of Arabia[129]?

Shahid No, D. H. Lawrence – he wrote a lot about physical passion[130] sex – 10

Riaz So did Barbara Cartland[131]. (*Addressing the others.*) See how calm I am?

They laugh.

Shahid (*continuing*) History shows that books can't be suppressed[132]. Dr Brownlow, surely you see how this is the road to dictatorship of the 15 mind, like in those Communist states.

Riaz That is presumption[133] and arrogance.

Shahid I am asking the brothers to consider that the telling of stories helps us all. It starts a conversation, however hard that may be.

Chad You agreeing with that blasphemer? 20

Shahid I am talking of what we need to do. As a poet yourself, brother Riaz –

Riaz This is not about us but the mind of the author –

Shahid And that mind you should defend!

Riaz This is the presumption I am talking of, brothers! 25

---

[127] John Milton (1608–1674): English poet – He published many pamphlets during the Civil War period, which advocated freedom of the press. His greatest works were the epic poems **Paradise Lost** (1667–1674), and **Paradise Regained** (1671) and the verse drama **Samson Agonistes** (1671).

[128] … New York: 500 copies of the novel were burned by New York postal officials in 1922.

[129] Lawrence of Arabia (1888–1935): Thomas Edward Lawrence, known as Lawrence of Arabia, British soldier and writer – He took a major part in the Arab revolt against the Turks (1916–1918). He described his experiences in **The Seven Pillars of Wisdom** (1926).

[130] passion: *Leidenschaft*

[131] Dame Mary Barbara Hamilton Cartland (1901–2000): English author of trivial literature, known for her numerous romantic best-selling novels

[132] to suppress: to prohibit, to prevent from publication

[133] presumption: bold and disrespectful behaviour

Shahid (*powering on*[134]) He[135] has said time and again he has your view of the world – the migrant's view. He celebrates what you are because out of you come new things.

Riaz There is nothing new after Allah's revelations.

5 **Shahid** But even these are not without dispute[136].

Riaz (*angry*) What do you mean?

Shahid (*overlapping*[137] *Riaz's question*) I have read the history. There were verses added to the Koran –

Riaz (*interjecting*[138]) – and refuted[139] by Allah himself as the work of

10 Satan!

Shahid But the fact of those verses remains. And if these were the work of Satan, you have to agree his mischief[140] made the faith stronger.

Riaz It enabled Allah to warn us about Satan, agreed.

Shahid Then can't you accept that the writer is also being playful, and

15 his new work will only make the faith stronger?

Riaz When there is so little known about us Muslims in public, we have a right to ensure[141] the *ummah*[142] – the Muslim community as a whole – is represented in ways that promote[143] all of us.

Brownlow (*to Shahid*) This is a n-n-new form of racism here, when

20 the Muslim working class is persecuted by middle-class, Cambridge types.

Shahid Aren't you being hypocritical[144], Dr Brownlow?

Brownlow I have never subscribed to[145] the British obsession[146] with class loyalty. We should seize this moment – for the first time under

25 Thatcher, there is the real possibility of persecuted classes making a difference. You have a cause, a passion that could place you in the vanguard[147] of changing this country!

---

[134] to power on: to become more energetic
[135] he: Rushdie
[136] dispute [dɪspjuːt]: disagreement
[137] to overlap: (here): to occur at the same time
[138] to interject: to interrupt what s.o. is saying with your remark
[139] to refute [riˈfjuːt]: to prove that s.th. is wrong
[140] mischief [ˈmɪs tʃɪf]: bad behaviour
[141] to ensure: to protect
[142] ummah (Arabic): the whole Muslim world
[143] to promote: to further the existence of s.th.
[144] hypocritical: *heuchlerisch*
[145] to subscribe to: to agree with or support
[146] obsession: s.th. you think about too much and too often
[147] vanguard: the leading position

Shahid Isn't it even more crucial[148] then that the cause is a right one?

Brownlow What matters is the commitment[149] to kick the old order out of its complacency[150]. Stand firm[151], Tariq – the new world order will be created by your class!

Shahid Literature is not a political party! Brother Riaz here is asking us   5 to become policemen of storytellers.

Riaz In these times, it is the duty of every Mussulman to become a policeman for his faith. The Ayatollah has made that very clear in his fatwa. He who does not act is not a true Muslim.

Shahid Brother Riaz, you asked me to prepare your poems for print.   10 You even accepted I could play with the words a little to make them fit today's way of speaking. Will playing with your words make me satanic in your eyes?

Riaz Forget this literature-shiterature talk. Let me ask you directly – if a character comes to your home in Sevenoaks and abuses[152] your   15 mother and sisters, what will you do?

Chad You got a problem, brother?

Shahid (*snaps*[153]) Don't call me brother! Why should you be more of a brother than any other man in the street?

Chad You confused, brother – (*To the others.*) Or he hiding something.   20

Riaz This writer has abused us in the same way that racist abused the old man and his family in the East End.

Shahid Do we have a monopoly on hurt? Why should our feelings of hurt be greater than his? If we attack him we become no better than the racists we oppose! We should debate with him. Censoring him   25 will only limit what we can be, when the whole world could be ours.

The door opens and Zulma enters.

Zulma Shahid – come. Attend[154], darling.

Shahid Auntie? This is a meeting!

Zulma I've told you before, don't call me Auntie! Sometimes censorship   30 is necessary! Who is in charge? (*to Riaz*) What are you doing, having a political meeting?

Riaz This is a private meeting, madam.

---

[148] crucial [ˈkruːʃl]: of great importance
[149] commitment: the willingness to work hard and give your energy and time to an activity
[150] complacency: feeling of extreme self-satisfaction
[151] firm: *fest*
[152] to abuse: to mistreat
[153] to snap: to speak with an angry, impatient voice
[154] attend: (here): Pay attention and listen to me!

Shahid We're discussing the *fatwa.*

Zulma And you're going to demonstrate in his favour?

Shahid No. Not in his favour, I don't think.

Zulma (*appalled*[155]) Students are supposed to have bloody brains, aren't
5   they?

Riaz Have some respect, madam.

Zulma Don't raise your voice to me! Religion is for the benefit[156] of the
masses, not for brainbox[157] types like you. Those simpletons[158] require
strict rules for living, otherwise they would still think the earth sits on
10   three fishes. But you mind-wallahs[159] must know it's a lot of balls[160].

Riaz (*controlling his ire*[161]) I am a peaceful man. I urge all to love those
of other religions, yes, even the wretched[162] Christ-killers[163] who lack
faith in their own faith. But we need to send a clear signal to everyone, Muslim and non-Muslim alike, that our faith is not a matter for
15   fictional debate.

Zulma Arey, practically the whole world is ringing me about this hullaballoo[164], as if I wrote the novel personally. Darling, things are getting
so extreme I may have to read it, and I only read on the toilet.

Riaz (*to the others*) Come, brothers, we have work to do.

20 *They leave, casting*[165] *murderous*[166] *glances at Zulma.*
   (*to Shahid, as he leaves*) I will pray Allah guides you to the true path,
   Shahid.

Zulma As if my head weren't burning up in flames with the problems
your entire family has given me, thank you very much.

25 *Shahid and Zulma are left alone.*
   Why are you in with those people? Oh, Shahid, what has happened
to you?

Shahid Please, Auntie, I need to think.

---

[155] appalled: shocked
[156] benefit: advantage, s.th. that improves
[157] brainbox (colloquial, BE): very intelligent
[158] simpleton: stupid person
[159] wallah (Hindi): a person connected with a certain job
[160] balls (slang): nonsense
[161] ire (formal): anger
[162] wretched: miserable
[163] Christ-killer (negative): Jew
[164] hullaballoo: loud, confused noise of protest
[165] to cast: to direct
[166] murderous: (here): very angry

Zulma You will certainly be needing to cogitate[167] after I give you one tight[168] slap.

Shahid You can't hit me.

Zulma Well, I'm in the mood. (*Tuts*[169].) You had a decent upbringing. And now I see you hanging round with beardies who've already messed up   5
Pakistan. I can't tell you the problems darling sweet Benazir Bhutto[170] is having with these tufty[171] cunts[172].

Shahid The problem is not people like Riaz, but your class, Zulma. You and your school friend Benazir, with your foreign bank accounts, doing nothing for the country but leeching[173] it for yourselves.   10

Zulma It's people like her who help maintain some decent image of the country abroad, darling. If it weren't for us, you'd see ZZ Top[174] on TV, and then where would we be?

Shahid Can you hear how arrogant you sound?

Zulma How dare you speak to me in that fashion? I thought you were   15
one notch[175] better than that brother of yours. You don't go in for prayers as well, do you? With that girl who should cover her whole bloody horse-face?

Shahid At least Tahira is not materialistic like you and Chili.

Zulma Let me tell you, next time I'm going to be demanding an arranged   20
marriage. These free marriages – what are they but bad manners in the day and bad smells at night? Oh, Shahid, we've not always been the best of friends, but it makes me feel rotten[176] to know you're running in that direction. They will slaughter[177] us soon for thinking. Have you stopped thinking, Shahid?   25

---

[167] to cogitate (formal): to think carefully about s.th.

[168] tight: (here): hard

[169] to tut: to make a disapproving sound

[170] Benazir Bhutto (1953–2007): Pakistani-born politician who was twice the Prime Minister of Pakistan (1988–1990 and 1993–1996) – She was assassinated in 2007. Her government was often accused of corruption.

[171] tufty: (here): having a short beard

[172] cunt (slang): (here) bastard

[173] to leech (fig.): to take the profit away from s.o.

[174] ZZ Top: white American hard rock band formed in 1969 that began to appear on MTV during the 1980s – Their musical style is considered root rock, i.e. a hybrid of folk, blues, and country music with the extensive use of electronic instruments. During the 1980s their music was especially popular because it contrasted with the widespread pop music at the time: new wave, punk rock, and heavy metal music.

[175] notch: (here): level

[176] rotten (colloquial): terrible

[177] to slaughter [ˈslɔːtə]: to kill like an animal

Shahid No.

Zulma Good. Then go back home at once and help your poor ammi.

Shahid I've got to finish my course! Papa wanted me to be educated.

Zulma Yes, he did. But you are spending all your time with those reli-
5   gious fools. Now you have to take charge of the family. When you see
that wasted brother of yours, be kind enough to inform him that his
place will be taken by you. Ring me when you get to Sevenoaks – I'm
going back to Karachi soon.

Shahid You can't put the mess of your married life on me, Auntie!

10 **Zulma** It's your family I'm thinking of – you have a duty to your ammi.
*Zulma storms out[178]. Shahid sits at his desk, finally alone. Puts up Riaz's
poem on his computer screen.*

THE MARTYR'S IMAGINATION
by Riaz al-Hussein

15   The windswept[179] sand speaks of adultery[180] in this godless land.
Here Lucifer and colonialists dance and Ibrahim[181] weeps when the
sun sets.
Wet bodies and captivating tongues reek of Satan's hot breath.
But Gibreel's fragrant green sword will veil the unveiled on the day
20   the sun finally sets.

*As he starts editing, we hear the sound of his fingers tapping[182] on the key-
board. This segues[183] into sounds of fists pounding[184] on desks.*

SCENE ELEVEN

*The canteen[185] at college. Fists pounding on desks and tables. Shahid en-
25 ters, sees Hat, who is with Tahira.*

Shahid What's happening?

Hat Democracy in action. Student protest full on.

---

[178] to storm out: to suddenly and angrily leave
[179] windswept: *windgepeitscht*
[180] adultery: *Ehebruch*
[181] Ibrahim (Arabic): Abraham
[182] to tap: to hit lightly
[183] to segue ['segweɪ]: to move smoothly from one activity to another
[184] to pound: to strike heavily and often
[185] canteen: *Mensa*

94

Shahid What about?

Hat This morning, that woman, Miss Osgood – she hold up the book.

Tahira That book. You hear?

Shahid (*sarky*) A book, in a college?

Hat I say, "Put down that book before I … You know what I'm saying, Miss 5
Deedee Osgood?" I say straight out, our parents pay taxes, here should
be British scholarship[186] and brainwaves[187], not curses[188]. She keep going,
"This is a classroom. There must be discussion, debate, argument!"

Shahid She's right …

Tahira Then we start fisting the desk. 10

Hat All the class take it up[189], smashing[190] down together.

Tahira Dr Brownlow say we have to be listened to. Our voices suppressed by Osgood types with the colonial mentality. To her we not
cool, we coolies[191].

Hat So Miss Deedee has to stick the book away[192] before someone sticks 15
it –

Tahira That pornographic priestess encourages brothers of colour to take
drugs. Then she force them into orgies. They tattoo[193] one another.

Hat (*curious*) With what?

Tahira Tattoo equipment. 20

Hat (*understanding*) I see.

Deedee enters in a rush.

Deedee (*to Hat*) Thanks for the protest, Hat. It's given me an idea for
a new course. (*To Shahid.*) "The History of Censorship and the
Importance of Immorality[194]." 25

Shahid Just what we need. How do we sign up?

Deedee Help me circulate[195] these leaflets[196].

She hands over some leaflets.

We're going to look at everyone from Plato[197] to Brecht[198] –

---

[186] scholarship: academic achievement, learning
[187] brainwave (colloquial, BE): good idea
[188] curse: obscene expression
[189] to take s.th. up: to join in doing s.th. that has already started
[190] to smash: to hit violently
[191] coolie: unskilled worker from Asia
[192] to stick away: to get rid of
[193] to tattoo: *tätowieren*
[194] immortality: *Unsterblichkeit*
[195] to circulate: to pass from person to person
[196] leaflet: pamphlet
[197] Plato (427 BC – 348 BC): classical Greek philosopher
[198] Bertold Brecht (1898–1956): German poet, playwright, theatre director

Tahira (*to Hat*) Yeah, the whole white doodah[199].

Deedee If anyone from your Nation of Islam's made a contribution to world literature, add them to the list. Can you think of anyone, Tahira?

5 *She stares at Tahira. A stand-off*[200]. *Chad enters, carrying a copy of* **The Satanic Verses**. *A beat. He exchanges looks with Deedee. And sees the leaflets in Shahid's hand.*

(*To Shahid.*) Get as many students as you can, Shahid.

Deedee exits. Chad snatches[201] *the leaflets from Shahid and flings*[202] *them*
10 *after her.*

Tahira Isn't it funny that nudists always keep their shoes on?

Chad Give me the stick, Hat.

Shahid You're a joker[203], man, if you think you're going to start beating people!

15 **Tahira** Yeah, just what she needs!

Chad (*to Hat*) The string, too! What you waiting for?

Shahid (*to Chad*) Listen Chad, that man, whatever he's done, he never called you Paki scum[204], did he?

Chad (*wound up*[205]) Shahid, I mean it – where are you spiritually[206],
20 man?

Shahid (*Considers*[207]. *Pause*) Chad, brother – I try never to do anything Prince wouldn't do.

Chad (*in his face*) Where's the typing we entrusted you with[208]?

Shahid I want to talk to brother Riaz.

25 **Chad** We had a talk and you left with that air hostess[209]! Brother Riaz more annoyed with you than ever.

Shahid Without Riaz, you're nothing.

Chad I agree with you.

Shahid You're a dog without a master.

30 **Chad** A dog, yeah?

---

[199] doodah (colloquial): anything you can't find a name for
[200] stand-off: deadlock, stalemate, a situation in which no agreement can be made
[201] to snatch: to seize suddenly
[202] to fling, flung, flung: to throw with force when you are angry
[203] joker (colloquial): stupid, silly person
[204] scum: trash, worthless person
[205] wound up: extremely nervous and tense
[206] spiritually: *geistig*
[207] to consider: to think carefully about a situation
[208] to entrust s.o. with s.th.: to put s.th. into s.o.'s care
[209] air hostess (ironic): stewardess

Chad chucks the book to Hat and pulls Shahid down by the wrists[210].

Shahid A dirty dog.

Chad Least I recognise that a master is required. Did I make the world? But I do know that I not a coward. Because you are always talking, never taking action! Because you always had a sitting-down life! That shit you told me the first day, you invent it to make yourself interesting! Actions will be taken!

Shahid Make sure they're the right actions.

Tahira (*intervening*[211]) This isn't the time for giving up, Shahid. Otherwise they'll put us in camps and turn on the gas.

Chad Don't forget the paraffin[212], Hat.

He pushes Shahid forward.

You in front with me.

He leads Shahid off into the courtyard. Hat has strung the book up[213] *and pours petrol on it. Riaz enters, followed by Brownlow, then Deedee.*

Deedee My God. What is happening to us? Shahid! Andrew! What's going on?

Brownlow's stutter prevents him answering.

Riaz Fellow students!

Deedee Are you going to burn that book, Riaz?

Riaz If you will permit me, in one moment I will explain.

Deedee Do you even know what that means?

Riaz Is the free speech of an Asian to be muzzled[214] by the authorities?

Various cries from the crowd around Riaz: "No, no."

"Let the brother speak!"

"His turn on the spot[215]*!"*

"Say it, brother!"

You understand? This is democracy!

Deedee (*incredulous*[216]) Democracy!

Riaz Are the white supremacists going to lecture[217] us on democracy this afternoon? Or will they permit us, for once, to practise it?

---

[210] wrist: *Handgelenk*
[211] to intervene: to take action to stop s.th. from continuing
[212] paraffin: oil used as a fuel for heat and light
[213] to string, strung, strung up: to hang in a high place with a string
[214] to muzzle: to prevent from being heard or noticed
[215] on the spot (colloquial): spot = spotlight – *im Rampenlicht*
[216] incredulous: unable to believe s.th.
[217] to lecture: *belehren*

Crowd cries: "Get off²¹⁸, white bitch²¹⁹!"
'Punk priestess!'

Deedee Why? Just explain why, Riaz?

Riaz To uphold values in our new society.

5 **Deedee** God save us from values!

Riaz You see? You see how feeble²²⁰ Christians are? A religion that's lost its hatred is not a religion – it is empty!

Deedee Then hooray for emptiness! My emptiness *is* the value. We've had too many values in Europe already. Doubt is our greatest need.

10 **Riaz** It's the sure road to filth! Filth like this book that people like you use to laugh at us. Well, it is time for your Western arrogance to understand it cannot interfere with God's decree²²¹.

Chad Jihad²²²!

Riaz Come, Shahid, take up your brother's cry. Look – the TV-wallahs
15 are here.

Shahid You called the press?

Riaz I listened to your advice.

As the crowd chants "Jihad! Jihad!" a Cameraman and Reporter take up positions, filming the action.

20 Let loose the piercing²²³ sword of truth!

Chad *Allah-u-Akbar²²⁴!*

Crowd *Allah-u-Akbar!*

Chad Don't mess with²²⁵ Muslims and their religion!

Deedee This can't happen!

25 *Deedee rushes out.*

Riaz *(to Shahid)* Consign²²⁶ this filth to the fate²²⁷ it deserves! Let the whole world see we shall not be overcome!

Reporter *(to Riaz)* Can you get a bit closer to the book?

---

²¹⁸ get off: stop interfering
²¹⁹ bitch: *Miststück*
²²⁰ feeble: very weak, with hardly any energy
²²¹ decree: official order from a ruler or government
²²² Jihad [dʒɪ ˈhæd] (Arabic): a holy war against infidels undertaken by Muslims in defence of the Islamic faith
²²³ to pierce: to force through with s.th. sharp
²²⁴ Allah-u-Akbar (Arabic): God is great.
²²⁵ to mess with: to get involved with s.o. or s.th. that may be harmful
²²⁶ to consign (formal): to hand over
²²⁷ fate: *Schicksal*

Riaz complies[228]. He signals to Chad, who tilts[229] the book while Hat thrusts[230] a lighter[231] into the pages.

Shahid No, Riaz!

Hat repeatedly tries to get the book to catch fire.

Hat The book too thick – he written too much.   5

Riaz Put more paraffin!

Shahid No!

Shahid rushes out, returning to his room, where he furiously[232] starts pounding on[233] his computer.

In the background, the book can be seen going up in flames[234]. Police si-   10
rens are heard, and Riaz and the gang scarper. Deedee is seen dousing[235] the burning book.

Shahid's typing gains[236] in volume[237].

Chili comes in, with Strapper in tow.

Chili Still working, bro?   15

Shahid (*flaring[238]*) I've got to be free to do what I want!

Chili Just a family enquiry[239], bro – chill[240]. (*To Strapper.*) Park yourself in the corner, Strap, and keep mum[241]!

They lie down, spaced out[242]. Shahid continues his work. We see him edit-ing Riaz's poem on his computer screen.   20

The Martyr's Imagination
by Riaz al-Hussein

---

[228] to comply: to obey an order

[229] to tilt: to move s.th. into a position so that one end is higher than the other

[230] to thrust: to push violently and suddenly

[231] lighter: anything that starts a fire

[232] furiously: with great anger

[233] to pound on: to hit s.th. hard several times

[234] going up in flames: On January 14, 1989 a group of angry Muslims took a copy of Sir Salman Rushdie's novel, **The Satanic Verses**, and burned it in front of Brad-ford City Hall. Two weeks afterwards, in Iran, the Ayatollah Khomeini declared a *fatwa* that demanded that Rushdie be killed because of the blasphemy he consid-ered to be in the novel.

[235] to douse: to stop a fire from burning by pouring water over it

[236] to gain: to increase

[237] volume: *Lautstärke*

[238] flaring: suddenly becoming angry

[239] enquiry: question to obtain information

[240] to chill (slang, AE): to relax

[241] to keep mum (colloquial): to remain quiet

[242] spaced out (colloquial): not completely conscious of what is happening around you because of drugs

The fire-swept[243] pavement[244] fizzes[245] treachery[246] in this green land.
Here Satan and Eve dance around the Martyr weeping into the setting sun.
Wet bodies and captivating tongues promise a paradise of pleasures,
5   But the curved green sword slices a curtain of certainty[247] down on the sun.

Scene Twelve

Shahid's digs. Evening. Chad, Hat and Tahira burst in. Shahid closes the document he's been working on.

10 **Chad** She against authority yet called police in! Brother Riaz has said that Osgood must be removed from her post for her attacks on minorities.

    Tahira And today she prevented our free expression. Isn't that racist censorship, Shahid?

15 **Shahid** You got your moment on TV.

    Hat She's left her office.

    Chad With my usual genius I've thought of what to do. Tonight we visit her private home.

    Shahid (*alarmed*) What?

20 **Chad** In order to learn, she must be taught a lesson.

    Chad signals to Hat to get the disc from Shahid's computer. Hat does so.

    Shahid What are you doing?

    Chad Riaz is waiting for us at the mosque.

    He snatches the disc from Hat.

25   I'm returning his property.

    Shahid (*reaches for it*) It's not finished.

    Chad It finished.

    He tosses[248] the disc to Hat.

    Check it out[249]. Go!

30 *Hat leaves.*

---

[243] fire-swept: with a fire rapidly moving through s.th.

[244] pavement (BE): part at the side of a road for people to walk on

[245] to fizz: to hiss

[246] treachery: betrayal, act of disloyalty

[247] certainty: state of being certain

[248] to toss: to throw carelessly

[249] to check out: to examine s.th. or look at s.th. to see if it is all right

(*Hauling*[250] *up the prone*[251] *Strapper*) And you, Mr Strapper, you're coming with us.

Strapper (*in a daze*[252]) What the – Hey, Trevor!

Chad I told you that's not my truth[253].

Strapper Where we going, man?   5

Chad To sniff her out[254]. Osgood – no good!

Tahira Osgood – no good! (*to Shahid*) You hear?

They leave. Chili stirs[255].

Shahid Come on, Chili – get yourself together!

Chili What fucking mess[256] you in, little brother?   10

Shahid We need to get to Deedee's.

Chili Never chase women.

Shahid cleans him up and pushes him forward out of the room. Chili turns back into the room.

Tonight I want a human touch. Decent bed. Clean sheets. Let's go to 15
her place and party, toot sweet!

Shahid Got your knife?

Chili (*flicks open*[257] *his knife*) You don't go round London without one.

Hat enters.

Hat (*in a state*[258], *to Shahid*) What you do that for, brother?   20

Chili Respect – that's my brother you talking to!

Shahid Where's my disc, Hat?

Hat You know what you've done.

Shahid No.

Hat I converted Riaz's poems on my printer.   25

Shahid Already?

Hat Yeah.

Shahid I see.

Hat I couldn't believe it!

Shahid I hadn't finished.   30

Hat Finished?

Shahid The poems –

---

[250] to haul: to pull s.th. or s.o. with a lot of effort
[251] prone (formal): lying flat with your face downwards
[252] in a daze: in a confused state
[253] truth: (here): reality
[254] to sniff out (colloquial): to find
[255] to stir: to move slightly
[256] mess: unpleasant situation
[257] to flick open: to open with a quick movement
[258] in a state: very excited and nervous

Hat How d'you think brother Riaz will feel, standing so proud and all, waiting for his rhymes to come out printed and clean so he could hold it in his hands and show his friends?

Shahid The original manuscript hasn't been touched.

5 **Hat** Him be shattered to pieces[259] when he sees this.

Shahid It's a celebration. Of passion.

Hat (*realises*) You been seeing that Miss Osgood, haven't you? And collaborating[260] with her all this time! You a raving[261] evil spirit and a double agent!

10 **Chili** For being with a woman?! (*to Shahid*) What friends you call these, bro?

Shahid Hat, did you like any of what I did?

Hat I can be a bit dirty-minded myself, but that stuff … You a sewer[262] rat. I don't go and put an essay on girls crossing their legs –

15 **Shahid** And on the smell of their hair, and on the skin behind their knees –

Hat Yeah! The odours[263] of their body and everything like that – people sniffing[264] one another's, you know, doodahs[265].

Shahid Didn't God give us our doodahs?

20 **Hat** I wouldn't put them into print and mix it up with religious words, would I?

Shahid I want us to be friends, Hat.

Hat Why rape[266] us then?

Chad You said that brother Riaz saved your life one time.

25 **Shahid** Yes.

Hat That why you turn on[267] him?

Shahid Hat, please believe me. I was just playing with words.

Hat Our religion isn't something you can test out, like trying on a suit to see if it fit!

30 **Shahid** Please, Hat, help me. I want to speak to Riaz alone. Just for half an hour. I want to explain everything. Will you talk to him without letting Chad know?

---

[259] shattered to pieces: extremely upset and shocked

[260] to collaborate: to work together with s.o. to achieve s.th.

[261] raving: talking in a way that shows s.o. is crazy

[262] sewer ['suːə]: *Abwasserkanal*

[263] odour ['əʊdə] (formal): smell, often unpleasant

[264] to sniff: to breathe air into your nose to discover the smell of s.th.

[265] doodah: (here): sex organ

[266] to rape: *vergewaltigen*

[267] to turn on s.o.: (here): to change your attitude towards s.o. and attack this person

Hat Brother Chad and all of us, we trusted you – apart from[268] Tahira, who say from the beginning you an egotist with an evil smile. And then Riaz put his soulful[269] words in your hands. It would have been a privilege for any of us! But he think you special. How can you think to bother[270] Riaz right now? He busy planning. 5

Shahid What?

Hat Just retributions[271].

Shahid Like what?

Hat I can't tell you.

Shahid Will you give me back the disc? 10

Hat I can't do that.

Shahid Then see you.

Hat Where you going?

Shahid pushes Hat out of the way. He falls. Shahid and Chili leave. Music, as they rush through London to Deedee's. 15

SCENE THIRTEEN

Deedee's house. Night. The TV is on. Shahid and Chili enter.

Shahid Where's Deedee? Where is she?

Brownlow Thankfully, I no longer care. Probably making a list of a few more names to slip[272] to the police. 20

Chili *(brandishing his knife)* Where's Strapper?

Shahid *(pushing Chili away)* Have you seen her?

Brownlow Finished rogering[273] my wife, Tariq? I imagined your religion frowned on[274] such things. Or have you had enough of her? Wouldn't blame you, sticking to your own. Especially with fiery[275] cadre[276] like 25 Tahira.

Shahid Is Deedee all right?

---

[268] apart from: except for
[269] soulful: expressing profound feelings
[270] to bother: *belästigen*
[271] retribution: severe punishment for a serious wrong that s.o. has done
[272] to slip: (here): to pass on secretly
[273] to roger (slang, BE): to have sex with a woman
[274] to frown on: to disapprove of s.th.
[275] fiery ['faɪəri]: passionate
[276] cadre: a person who is a member of a specially trained group, especially one that is military

Brownlow "LBJ, LBJ, how many kids you burned today?"[277]

Chili Who's burning kids?

Brownlow That was our chant at Cambridge[278] in the sixties when students were a united force, pissing on the gods of authority. Now you
5 guys, in the most reactionary period since the war, have picked up the baton[279].

Shahid But you're out of it, aren't you? You're fucking off[280], leaving everything.

Brownlow What's there to teach when there is no longer any knowledge
10 to transmit[281]? I'm off to Italy. Or France. Or maybe Spain. What does it matter? Everyone's standing by their own miserable class or race. Rudder's going to say the book's an insult and call for it to be withdrawn[282]. The Tory leader's agreed to do the same.

Shahid What the fuck for?

15 **Brownlow** Don't be naive, there's a lot of Asian votes to be had round there. *(Ironic.)* Up the revolution! Did I tell you, Riaz has been invited on *Newsnight*[283] to give his opinion on the *fatwa*?

Shahid Stop pissing me about[284]!

Brownlow Don't know who's pissing whom.

20 **Chili** Any booze[285] in the house?

Brownlow *(to Shahid, referring to Chili)* I see you're enjoying a different class of friend, Tariq.

Chili Tosser[286].

Brownlow *(to Shahid)* Riaz's eyes went all bright[287] when he heard. He'll
25 make a fascinating freak[288] on TV. For a week or month. Just when you thought God was dead and buried, you realise he was merely awaiting

---

277 LBJ ... burned today?: a chant used by protesters of the Vietnam War in America during the late 1960s – LBJ (Lyndon Baines Johnson) was president at the time (1963–1969). The burning is a reference to the widespread use of napalm fire-bombs in Vietnam.
278 Cambridge: Cambridge University
279 to pick up the baton ['bætɒn] (short stick used in a relay race): to take over an activity from s.o. before you
280 out of it ... off: no longer involved
281 to transmit: to pass on
282 to withdraw: to ban
283 Newsnight: BBC Television current affairs programme since 1980
284 to piss about (slang): to treat s.o. in a way that seems silly and a waste of time
285 booze (slang): alcoholic drink
286 tosser (slang, BE): stupid, unpleasant person
287 to go bright: to become all shiny
288 freak: bizarre person

resurrection[289]! Every fucker's[290] discovering some god inside them now. Who am I to challenge this?

Shahid Help us find Deedee!

Brownlow There we were, right up to the end of the seventies, arguing about society after the revolution, and all the while it was being taken from us. The British people don't want education, arts, justice, equality … Everything I believed has turned into shit.

Shahid You're a spineless[291] bastard.

Brownlow I've been called worse, Tariq.

Shahid (*pushing him*) My name is Shahid!

Chili That's – manly – bro.

Brownlow (*leaving*) Look – no stutter, see?

Brownlow exits.

Shahid (*shouting*) Deedee!

Chili Ahh, soft, bro – always call a woman softly …

Deedee enters from the kitchen.

Deedee What more do you want, Andrew …? (*Sees Shahid and Chili.*) What're you doing here?

Shahid We've been looking everywhere for you.

Deedee Did Andrew let you in?

Shahid Forget it. Chad and the others know where you live.

Deedee What?

Shahid They're out for revenge[292]. They're coming for you. Me too, now.

Deedee Will you talk sense!

Shahid You called in the police and I fucked around[293] with their master's words.

Deedee looks at him quizzically[294].

   I rewrote some of Riaz's poetry. Didn't mean to. I was just playing as I was thinking of you – to see where it would take me. I was going to change it back. Riaz and the gang think it's blasphemy.

Deedee They're coming here?

---

[289] resurrection: returning to life again after being dead
[290] fucker: (slang): bastard
[291] spineless: without a spine (*Rückgrat*)
[292] revenge: *Rache*
[293] to fuck around: to alter in an undesirable way
[294] quizzically: in a puzzled manner

Chili Any booze in the house? I need a pick-me-up[295]. Booze and a little nap[296], yeah, just a little sleep.

Deedee (*to Shahid*) And you've brought him – (*indicating Chili*) – to help?

5 *Chili puts his arms around Deedee and whispers. Deedee laughs.*

Shahid (*tetchy*) Chili.

Deedee (*to Shahid*) Your big brother wants to put my tits[297] in his mouth.

Chili It's worth trying.

10 **Shahid** Chili!

Chili I'm lonely, all right? Tonight I want a human touch. To feel warm skin. Is that too much to ask? (*to Shahid*) All right, all right. (*to Deedee*) Any drink in the house, Deedee Osgood? Then I'm ready to take on[298] any fucker who comes to annoy you. Me and my bottle

15 will stand guard on the stairs. That's where the enemy will come in, through the upstairs windows!

Shahid Make sure you lock it – and the back door.

Chili Toot sweet, bro, toot sweet. – Where's your back door, Deedee?

Deedee Fuck it[299] if they're going to make me a prisoner in my own

20 house. I'm going to cook. (*taking Chili*) Come on, let's find a bottle for you.

Deedee takes Chili off[300]. The door rattles[301].

Strapper (*off*) It's only me, Strapper, the Strap. Official visit, man.

Shahid opens the front door. Strapper strolls[302] in.

25 **Shahid** I thought you were with your old pal Trevor.

Strapper Chad's a religious type, he see everything from underneath. You just wanna be white and forget your own. (*He shouts.*) You and your bro just wanna shag the white bitches! That why he don't go for you no more.

30 **Shahid** I wish I hadn't let you in.

Strapper How were you gonna[303] keep me out, cunt? Hey, don't touch me, man.

---

[295] pick-me-up: drink that restores your energy
[296] nap: short, light sleep
[297] tits (slang): breasts
[298] to take on: to oppose, to fight
[299] fuck it: (slang): *Scheiße!*
[300] off: off stage
[301] to rattle: to make a series of short, loud sounds when hitting against s.th. hard
[302] to stroll [strəʊl]: to walk in a relaxed way
[303] gonna (slang): going to

Shahid Get out of here.

Strapper The brothers burned the book, right? Funny how you people get into more of a state[304] about a book than about the suffering people.

Shahid (*pushing him towards the door*) You're making me suffer now, Strapper.   5

Strapper I wouldn't get heavy[305]. Thing is, brown boy, your Chili owes me money. Where's he hiding round here?

He suddenly jumps and holds the front door wide open.

(*Shouts in a military voice.*) All clear!   10

Chad, Tahira and Hat enter.

Shahid You bastard!

Chad grabs Shahid in an armhold[306] and offers him to Hat, while Strapper looks on.

Chad Here's the scum, as expected – holed up[307] with his bitch. So obvi-   15
ous. Now, brothers, get to work on the spy, the infidel[308], the traitor[309]! Go on. Go on.

Hat But me papa will be looking for me!

Chad Your father? What's he got to do with this?

Hat I can't stay.   20

Chad Beat him! This idiot hates us and he hates God! Give Satan one!

Tahira Satan! Satan!

Tahira knees Shahid in the crotch[310] and repeatedly boots[311] him.

Chad The evil spirit has gone down!

Shahid staggers[312] up. Tahira kicks him again. Deedee runs in.   25

Deedee Leave him!

Chad (*bars[313] her way*) He belong to us now. Let us take him, bitch, and there'll be no trouble for you! We're going to deal with the spy.

Tahira He deceived[314] and spat[315] on his own, wallowing[316] in filth.

---

[304] a state: a state of anger and excitement
[305] heavy (slang): unpleasant
[306] armhold: with the arms around s.o.'s body
[307] holed up: hiding somewhere
[308] infidel: non-believer
[309] traitor: *Verräter, -in*
[310] crotch: the part of the body where the legs join at the top
[311] to boot: to kick hard with your foot
[312] to stagger: to walk unsteadily as if about to fall
[313] to bar s.o.'s way: to block s.o.'s way
[314] to deceive: to trick, to make s.o. believe s.th. that's not true
[315] to spit, spat, spat: *spucken*
[316] to wallow: to lie and roll about in s.th. (said of animals)

Deedee Let go of him!

Chad Eye for an eye – that so hard to understand, Miss Post-Colonial Studies?

Deedee Very cute[317], Mr Trevor.

5 **Chad** (*raises his hand to strike her*) Don't use that name on me!

Deedee (*jibing*) What's wrong, Mohammad Shahabuddin Ali-Shah?

Riaz enters.

Chad Here he is. Sick, sick, sick as you prophesied.

Tahira More sick now.

10 **Chad** We've captured both of them! What now, brother? What action to take immediately? Which step do you want? Shall we take him away? Or finish him here?

Riaz (*to Shahid*) You've pierced my heart, Shahid … Do you want to stand always alone? Or be one with the *ummah* that is your heart's

15 only family?

Shahid I'll find my own *ummah*, thanks.

Riaz Bring him for interrogation[318]! We will purify those who cannot purify themselves. He must be shown the raging[319] fires of hell.

He turns to lead them out.

20 **Hat** (*in horror*) Brothers! It that maniac[320]!

Chili stands on the stairs above them, brandishing his knife.

Chili Hello, all. Robert De Niro's[321] waiting.

Strapper Chili-boy!

Chili O ye[322] of little faith[323], Strap!

25 **Strapper** (*jigging[324] furiously*) It's going up[325], it's going up! Fuck everything! Fuck you all!

Chad Right! We'll halal[326] them all now.

He squares up[327] to Chili.

---

[317] cute [kjuːt] (colloquial, AE): clever in an annoying way

[318] interrogation: *Verhör, Vernehmung*

[319] raging: moving up with great violence

[320] maniac ['meɪniæk]: madman

[321] Robert De Niro (1943–   ): American actor and film director who often plays criminals

[322] ye (old-fashioned): you

[323] O ye of little faith …: This phase appears several times in the New Testament, e.g. Matthew 6:30.

[324] to jig: to move up and down with short quick movements

[325] It's going up!: It's going up in smoke.: Everything is turning disastrous.

[326] to halal (Arabic): to slaughter an animal according to Muslim law

[327] to square up to s.o.: to face s.o. ready to fight

Chili Yeah? I don't like kosher[328] meat.

Chili flies into the gang, knocking Chad, Tahira and Hat out of the way and grabs Riaz, holding the knife to his throat.

    (*To the others.*) Now fuck off, all of you! Or else this brother gets halal-ed.   5

Riaz (*terrified*) Go, go.

Chad Leave him! Or you get it[329]!

Chad takes a step forward, Chili touches Riaz with the knife and Riaz bleeds. Chad stops.

Chili (*to Riaz*) And get this fucking shirt off! I told you it were mine, 10
man, now give it back.

Riaz, confused, looks to Chad.

    Now!

Riaz takes off the shirt.

Chad I'll halal you for this, I swear[330].   15

Chili Yeah, yeah. Bigger boys than you have tried to take on Chili. (*to Riaz*) Pants too.

Riaz complies.

Chad You an evil spirit – how can you make brother Riaz change in front of women?   20

Chili He got something he ain't proud of? (*to Riaz*) My fucking socks as well!

Riaz is forced to complete the undressing.

Chad You goin' straight to hell!

Chili Just the place I want! Care to join me there? Now fuck off out of 25
here with your poodles[331]! Then I'll release[332] this one!

Chad There are hundreds like us, hundreds and thousands!

Chili What you waiting for – bring them on!

They go, and Chili flings Riaz out.

Riaz We will start another experiment, *insha' Allah*[333]!   30

Chili Yeah, yeah.

Deedee (*concerned*[334]) Shahid …

Shahid I'm all right. Really.

---

[328] kosher [ˈkəʊʃə] (Yiddish): slaughtered according to Jewish law
[329] get it: get killed
[330] to swear [sweə]: *schwören*
[331] poodle (colloquial, BE): a person who is too willing to do what s.o. else tells them to do
[332] to release: to let go
[333] insha' Allah (Arabic): God willing
[334] concerned: worried

Deedee Time we had a proper meal.

Chili I've had all I can stomach, babe[335].

A beat.

Deedee Take care of yourself, Chili.

5 *Deedee goes to the kitchen.*

Chili (*to Shahid*) Hug[336] me, bro.

They embrace[337].

Shahid Thanks for saving my balls[338].

Chili Cool entrance, eh? Someone should have videoed it. You okay?

10 **Shahid** Sore[339] all over. Going somewhere?

Chili nods[340].

    With Strapper?

Chili Yeah.

Shahid After what he did?

15 **Chili** Will you talk to Ammi for me? Say I'm okay? Getting better? You know what to say.

Shahid Toot sweet, brother.

Chili Yeah.

Chili exits, with Strapper. Deedee leaves the room.

20 *There is a tapping on the window. Shahid grabs a knife and investigates[341].*
Hat is knocking. Shahid opens the window.

Hat Will you listen if I say something? Please, Shahid.

Shahid Why should I trust you?

Hat I trying to say I sorry about what happened.

25 **Shahid** Oh, yeah.

Hat Please listen! There's no one else – I alone! Because Allah is forgiving and merciful,[342] I will only show love and consideration[343] for others. I ashamed of what we did.

Shahid Why?

30 **Hat** Whatever you done, it not my place to condemn another person. Only God can do that. I was wrong to put myself in that position, as if I never done wrong things. I hope you don't turn away from Allah.

---

[335] babe (slang): a way to address a young woman, wife, girlfriend, etc.
[336] to hug: to put your arms around s.o. to show you love or like s.o.
[337] to embrace: to hug
[338] balls (slang): *Hoden* – (here): life
[339] sore: painful
[340] to nod: to move your head up and down to show you agree
[341] to investigate: to examine a situation
[342] merciful: showing mercy (*Gnade*)
[343] consideration: the quality of thinking about another person's feelings and wishes

Shahid To tell you the truth, Hat – I'm sick of being bossed around, whether by Riaz or Chad or God himself. Brother, what we do, and the things we make, is more interesting than anything that God is supposed to have done. Do your accountancy[344], Hat. You'll regret it if you don't pass. 5

Hat I disagree. But I get what you say. I said what I have to.

He starts to leave.

Shahid Where are you going?

Hat To paradise. Please forgive me. Forgive all of us and may there be mercy. 10

Hat leaves. Deedee enters.

Shahid I want to be with you.

Deedee For as long as it lasts?

Shahid For as long as that.

They embrace. 15

A beat.

Dawn. Hat is seen carrying a rucksack. He bends down to take it off his shoulders. An explosion. Hat is killed. Sounds of sirens. Ambulances, fire engines, police cars and flashing[345] lights.

Deedee and Shahid go out. There is a pall[346] of smoke. 20

Shahid and Deedee look at each other.

Shahid I want to see my mother. Come with me? Then we can go to the sea – I know a place. I've decided. I know what to write.

She holds out her hand. He takes it and they walk off, towards the dawn[347]. 25

Mobile phones start ringing, coalescing[348] into sounds of wild celebrations at news of London winning the 2012 Olympics. Four young men appear, wearing baseball caps and with rucksacks slung[349] on their backs. Blackout[350].

---

[344] accountancy: the necessary training to become an accountant
[345] to flash: to shine very brightly for a short time
[346] pall: thick, dark cloud
[347] dawn: sunrise
[348] to coalesce[ˌkəʊəˈles]: to come together to form one mass
[349] to sling, slung, slung: to hang loosely
[350] blackout: all the lights on the stage are shut off

Information Box

2012 Olympics and 7/7

The announcement, however, that London had been selected for the 2012 Olympics was not made until 6 July 2005. One day later the London bombings of 7 July 2005 (often referred to as 7/7) took place. It was a series of coordinated suicide attacks upon Londoners using the public transport system during the morning rush hour. During that morning, four militants detonated four bombs, three on London Underground trains in quick succession, a fourth bomb exploding an hour later in a double-decker bus in Tavistock Square, London. Fifty-six people, including the four bombers, were killed by the attacks, and about 700 were injured. Three of the bombers were of Pakistani descent and all were motivated by Islamic extremism that includes the belief that a suicide bomber will end up in paradise. Why do you think the playwright uses this anachronism at the end of his play, although the time of the play is at the end of the 1980s?

Pakistani Migration and Diaspora
by Pnina Werbner

Pakistanis form a global diaspora[1] that emerged[2] after World War II, following the partition of India and Pakistan in 1947. Major concentrations
of Pakistanis exist in the United States, Canada, and Norway, and small- 5
er Pakistani communities are also to be found in most Western European
countries, in Australia, and in postcolonial[3] developing countries, especially the Middle East and Gulf States, Malaysia, Indonesia, and East
and southern Africa (where many arrived before partition). [...]

Migrants from the Indian subcontinent, among them Pakistanis, be- 10
gan arriving in Britain in substantial numbers after World War II. They
were recruited to assist with the reconstruction of the British economy,
entering low-skilled jobs abandoned by the local population in the post-
war boom years. The initial migration was of single young men, usually originating from smallholder peasant[4] farms in the Punjab[5]. Many of 15
the earliest arrivals were East Punjabis from the more developed, highly
populated regions of Jullundur and Hoshiapur (now in India), which
suffered from chronic land shortages and boasted[6] better educational facilities. A major stream of arrivals in the early years were students from
this region studying at British universities. Most factory workers arrived 20
through chain migration, following in the footsteps of relatives or co-
villagers, but many were also recruited by agents who found them jobs
in the British economy. The early arrivals were, on the whole, relatively
skilled and educated, at least to the primary or high school level. Some
had served in the Indian or Pakistani armies, and others had worked in 25
factories in Pakistan or India prior to[7] their arrival.

The Pakistani diaspora in Britain can only be understood fully in
terms of its national origins in Pakistan, a postcolonial nation created
during the final years of British colonial rule in India. The partition of

---

[1] diaspora [daɪˈæspərə]: the massive movement of the people of a nation to other countries
[2] to emerge: to start to exist
[3] postcolonial: occurring after the break-up of the British Empire
[4] peasant farmer: poor farmer who usually doesn't own the land
[5] Punjab: province of Pakistan
[6] to boast: (here): to have (seen as s.th. very positive)
[7] prior to: before

British India in 1947 came as a reluctant capitulation to[8] the demands of the Muslims of India for national autonomy. [...]

Despite the traumatic events of partition, a shared history and culture mean that Pakistanis in Britain cannot be thought of apart from the broader South Asian diaspora. Moreover, their relationship with Britain as their former colonial master colours first-generation migrants' oppositional diasporic sensibility[9], while creating common ground (in their shared knowledge of English, love of cricket, and respect for democratic institutions) for mutual regard and understanding. Overseas South Asians in Britain and elsewhere need to be understood as forming a complex, segmented diaspora composed of four nationalities (Indian, Pakistan, Bangladeshi, and Sri Lankan), four major religions (Islam, Hinduism, Sikhism, and Christianity, along with some Buddhists), and a multiplicity of languages and regional popular cultures. [...]

During the 1960s, a stream of migrants continued to arrive from West Punjab [in Pakistan] [...]. These migrants, too, originated mainly from smallholder[10] peasant farms [...] Many came from impoverished[11] backgrounds [and] settled in northern towns, working in the ailing[12] wool and cotton mills of Yorkshire and Lancashire. Indeed, they propped up this industry for some 20 years before it finally collapsed. [...]

In the early stages, Pakistani migrants concentrated in large numbers in regions of Britain that were suffering from acute[13] labour shortages, mainly the West Midlands, Yorkshire, and Lancashire, and in cities such as Birmingham, Bradford, Manchester, Newcastle-on-Tyne, and Glasgow in Scotland. [...] South Asian trading communities also emerged in most major cities, serving the culinary[14] and other ethnic consumer demands of the growing migrant population, and establishing many other small businesses, particularly in the clothing and textile trades. [...]

Broadly speaking, by 2001, Pakistanis were more concentrated in the north and west Midlands, East Africans and Indians in the east Midlands and the outer London area [...]

The tightening of immigration laws affected patterns of migration to Britain. Initially, migrants from the subcontinent were defined as British subjects and were free to enter the country at will. In 1962, a work

---

[8] capitulation to: giving in to, surrender to
[9] sensibility. (here): attitudes
[10] smallholder (BE): a person who owns or rents a small piece of land for farming
[11] impoverished: extremely poor
[12] ailing: having problems without much hope for the future
[13] acute: (here): very high
[14] culinary: restaurant and food

voucher[15] scheme was introduced, limiting migration, and although initially, this accelerated the scale of male migration, after 1969 migration was restricted to incoming marriage partners and nuclear family[16] reunions, including children under the age of 18. Pakistan allows dual nationality, and after 1969, most Pakistani migrants working in Britain applied for British passports and began to bring over their wives and children for fear they might lose their entitlement to[17] British citizenship. What had initially begun as a pattern of circulatory labour migration, with young migrant men expecting to come to Britain to work for short periods to save money before returning home, turned into a process of permanent settlement. [...]

Most first-generation Pakistani entrepreneurs began as factory workers, accumulating some of the startup funds needed. These were augmented[18] by an institutionalised system of long-term, interest-free loans between fellow migrants, money saved (often by wives) in rotating credit associations known as *kommitti*, and, in the food and clothing industries, by credit extended to new retailers by established South Asian wholesalers[19]. Business niches included, in the first instance, the ethnic grocery food and halal[20] trade, "Indian" restaurants, and South Asian fabric shops and travel agents. From the start, Pakistanis in major conurbations[21] also began marketing ready-to-wear garments[22] in open-air markets, as well as wholesaling, and manufacturing cheap clothing. These enterprises relied on the existence of a pool of cheap labour, including family labour. Some firms, such as Joe Bloggs, based in Manchester, have become giant multimillion concerns with their own brand names. [...]

In addition to food, housing, clothing, and textiles, Pakistanis have also carved out[23] a niche in transport, and in many towns they dominate or have a large share of the taxi-driving business. [...] Taxi driving is a lucrative, flexible, but highly risky business: Passengers may be violent or racist, and there have been several cases of murders. Nevertheless, young Pakistanis without formal qualifications can find work within

---

[15] work voucher ['vaʊtʃə]: document proving you have a job offer
[16] nuclear family: mother, father and children
[17] entitlement to: right to
[18] to augment: to increase
[19] wholesaler: *Großhändler*
[20] halal (Arabic): the slaughtering of animals for food according to Islamic law
[21] conurbation: large area where various towns have grown together, especially around large cities
[22] garments: clothing
[23] to carve out: to establish with hard work

the ethnic economy as taxi drivers, waiters, overlookers[24], packers, and clothing machinists. There is some evidence that a few South Asians have also entered crime, protectionism, and racketeering[25], including drug and human trafficking, although they by no means dominate this
5 trade.

Islam and The Rushdie Affair

[...]
   Until the publication of **The Satanic Verses**, Muslims in Britain were perceived as a law-abiding[26] minority. The diasporic public sphere that
10 they had evolved[27], although critical of India, Pakistan, Arab regimes, and the West, was local and hidden, invisible to outsiders. Pakistanis were often locked in the early settlement period in fratricidal[28] factional disputes in central mosques, and divided into tiny, fragmented *tonga* voluntary organisations. It was difficult to imagine their mobilisation as
15 a united front. The global crisis that came to be known as the Rushdie affair, with book burning in Bradford[29] screened on TV worldwide, and the death sentence *fatwa* pronounced by the Ayatollah Khomeini, which caused a major international rupture[30] between Iran and the West, brought this subterranean[31] Muslim local-level politics into the public
20 eye.
   The Satanic Verses, a novel written by an eminent diasporic Pakistani author living in London, Salman Rushdie, was an iconoclastic[32] critique of Islamic fundamentalism and of Thatcherite[33] Britain, and was part of

---

[24] overlooker: overseer, i.e. a person who watches over other people to make sure they work properly
[25] racketeering: illegal activities
[26] law-abiding: obeying the law
[27] to evolve: to slowly develop
[28] fratricidal: having to do with killing your brother
[29] Bradford: On January 14, 1989 a group of angry Muslims took a copy of Sir Salman Rushdie's novel, **The Satanic Verses**, and burned it in front of Bradford City Hall. Two weeks later, in Iran, the Ayatollah Khomeini declared a *fatwa*, demanding that Rushdie be killed because of the blasphemy he perceived in **The Satanic Verses**.
[30] rupture: disruption
[31] subterranean: hidden from the public eye
[32] iconoclastic: attacking traditional or established concepts
[33] Thatcherite: during the time of Prime Minister Margaret Thatcher (1925–   ) from 1979 to 1990, whose Conservative government was very pro-business and anti-union

a broader South Asian postcolonial literary movement that has created a culturally hybrid[34] form of the English novel. The novel was regarded by most Pakistanis in Britain, and by Muslims worldwide, as highly offensive[35]. It led to a *fatwa* by the Ayatollah Khomeini of Iran, denouncing the author as an apostate[36] and sentencing[37] him to death. The ensuing[38] international crisis led to a radical change in the public political activism of Pakistanis in Britain. A large anti-Rushdie demonstration in London in 1989 mobilised Muslims, primarily South Asians, across the different sectarian[39] and organisational divides.

This process of becoming more visible has continued. Since the Rushdie affair, a series of other international crises has disrupted the processes of Pakistani integration into Britain and induced a sense of widening alienation[40]. The 1991 Gulf War, the conflicts in Bosnia, Palestine, Kashmir, and Chechnya, the events of and subsequent to[41] 11 September 2001, the nuclear confrontation between India and Pakistan, and the wars in Afghanistan and Iraq have all mobilised Pakistanis and other Muslims onto the streets of Britain, with Muslim representatives regularly invited to Downing Street and Muslim MPs openly protesting against the war in Afghanistan.

Historically, then, as in the case of many immigrant settler groups in the religiously plural West, Islam began for South Asian Muslims arriving in Britain in the postwar era as an acceptable, legitimate incorporative[42] identity, non-racialised, highly cultural, and highly valorised[43]. The mosque was the central locus[44] of cultural value, the focus of communal factional[45] politics, a point of mobilisation, a haven[46] for incoming migrants, and a basis for solidarity in times of crisis. It provided a

---

[34] hybrid (literary term): mixture of cultures
[35] offensive: insulting
[36] apostate: s.o. who abandons his/her religion
[37] to sentence: *verurteilen*
[38] ensuing: following
[39] sectarian: religious
[40] alienation: feeling that you don't belong to a society
[41] subsequent to: after
[42] incorporative: forming a unity
[43] valorised: valued, considered in a positive light
[44] locus (Latin): place
[45] factional: party
[46] haven: safe and protected place

platform for subaltern[47] orators and lay preachers[48] excluded from formal British political arenas.

Since the Rushdie affair and even more since 11 September, [...] Islam has become a flag of political dissent. The growth of specifically anti-
5 Muslim prejudice, Islamophobia, has exacerbated[49] this process. So, too, has the related perception that mosques are sites of rhetorical vilification[50] of the West and, in a few cases, of incitement[51] to terror. Stripped[52] of its experiential dimensions[53], beyond personal belief, Islam is now an oppositional badge[54]. One may speak of an identity-led religiosity. This
10 has led to a serious questioning in the British press and media of the loyalty of young, second-generation British Muslims and the extent[55] of their identification with British society.

In this context first- and second-generation Pakistanis, men and women alike, are increasingly adopting Islamic diacritical[56] ritual em-
15 blems and practices, which act as boundary markers, setting them apart from non-Muslim youngsters, including other young South Asians. Whereas the North Indian Islam of the migrant generation, embed-ded[57] in Sufi[58] traditions, tended to be relatively relaxed, with veiling[59] and *purdah*[60] abandoned in large measure by the Muslim middle classes
20 when they settled in Britain, in contemporary Britain the wearing by women of *burqas*[61], elaborate veils, and North African style headscarves by women, and of beards by men, is linked to a total abstinence from[62]

---

[47] subaltern (literary term): belonging to a people formally ruled by the British during the time of the British Empire
[48] lay preacher: *Laienprediger*
[49] to exacerbate: to make worse
[50] vilification: using hateful language to make s.th. or s.o. look bad
[51] incitement: the act of provoking
[52] stripped: completely removed
[53] experiential dimensions: aspects of religion whereby you participate in religious ceremonies or apply your religious beliefs to everyday life
[54] badge: (here): special form of a religion that you are proud to associate with
[55] extent: degree *(Ausmaß)*
[56] diacritical: distinctive, showing a difference
[57] embedded: with deep roots in
[58] Sufi: a variety of Muslim religion that emphasises the simple life and a direct relationship to God
[59] to veil [veɪl]: to use a veil *(Schleier)*
[60] purdah: keeping women in houses and requiring them to cover their whole body when going out
[61] burqa (Arabic): a loose dress that covers the complete body of a woman, including the face
[62] abstinence from: completely staying away from s.th.

drinking alcohol and a refusal to participate in British youth and student clubbing culture, which celebrates music, dance, sexuality, drink, and drugs.

This has led to a political discourse[63] that accuses Muslims of self-segregation, while Sikh and Hindu youngsters appear increasingly well integrated, although evidence exists that they, too, sometimes support extremist nationalist movements. Despite these accusations, young Pakistanis are, nevertheless, very British. [...]

However, the predicament[64] of the Muslim diaspora in Britain has been that, rather than gradual integration, with Islam accorded[65] respect as a religion of tolerance and peace, the community has been unable to escape the stigma generated by international conflicts with their globally transmitted[66] images of book- or effigy[67]-burning Muslim mobs. Conflicts of identification create tragic dilemmas for diasporas, which are, by definition, transnational[68] communities of co-responsibility[69]. Pakistanis in Britain identify deeply with the plight[70] of Palestinians, Bosnians, Kashmiris, Afghans, and Iraqis. They see the West, and especially the United States, as an oppressor. The result has been that rather than peaceful integration, the Muslim diaspora community in Britain has had to lurch[71] from one crisis to another, from the Rushdie affair to the Gulf War to 9-11. The images of alienation these conflicts have generated have been exacerbated by the inner-city rioting of young Pakistanis in northern British towns and by the revelation[72] that some young British Muslims have joined the Taliban and other extremist groups.

[Nevertheless] [...] Pakistanis in Britain have remained, on the whole, peaceful and pragmatic. Islam is a congregational[73] religion, which provides a valued identity for immigrants. Much of it is home-based, focused around rites of passage[74] or communal Koran readings, which mobilise family and friends. [...] There is little or no *purdah* practiced in homes,

---

[63] discourse: discussion
[64] predicament: difficult situation
[65] accorded: given, granted
[66] to transmit: to send via radio waves
[67] effigy: a doll, or image of s.o.
[68] transnational: involving several countries
[69] co-responsibility: the state of being responsible for one another
[70] plight: difficult situation
[71] to lurch: to move suddenly from one position to another
[72] revelation: showing s.th. that has been hidden or unknown before
[73] congregational: with an organised structure that brings people together
[74] rite of passage: a ceremony that celebrates important moments in a person's life

beyond formal etiquette. Most second-generation women move around freely, drive and work in salaried employment. They are active in their own philanthropic voluntary associations and have their own religious experts. The younger generation, both men and women, is currently entering the open job market in large numbers. For many, Islam appears to be an adventure of self-discovery, an enjoyable substitute for British youth culture.

from **Encyclopedia of Refugee Cultures Around the World, Volume One**, Melvin Ember, Carol R. Ember, Ian Skoggard, editors, Springer Science + Business Media, Inc., New York, 2005, pp. 475–484

Prime Minister Tony Blair's Speech on the London Bombing

16 July 2005

The greatest danger is that we fail to face up to the nature of the threat we are dealing with. What we witnessed in London last Thursday week ⁵ was not an aberrant[1] act.

It was not random[2]. It was not a product of particular local circumstances in West Yorkshire.

Senseless though any such horrible murder is, it was not without sense for its organisers. It had a purpose. It was done according to a plan. It ¹⁰ was meant.

What we are confronting here is an evil ideology.

It is not a clash of civilisations – all civilised people, Muslim or other, feel revulsion[3] at it. But it is a global struggle and it is a battle of ideas, hearts and minds, both within Islam and outside it. ¹⁵

This is the battle that must be won, a battle not just about the terrorist methods but their views. Not just their barbaric acts, but their barbaric ideas. Not only what they do but what they think and the thinking they would impose on[4] others.

Religious ideology ²⁰

This ideology and the violence that is inherent[5] in it did not start a few years ago in response to a particular policy. Over the past 12 years, Al-Qaeda and its associates have attacked 26 countries, killed thousands of people, many of them Muslims.

They have networks in virtually every major country and thousands ²⁵ of fellow travellers[6]. They are well-financed. Look at their websites.

They aren't unsophisticated[7] in their propaganda. They recruit, however, and whoever they can and with success.

---

[1] aberrant: not normal or right
[2] random: with no prearranged plan
[3] revulsion: strong feeling of disgust
[4] to impose on: to force on s.o.
[5] inherent: existing as an inseparable part
[6] fellow traveller: someone who sympathises with a political movement
[7] unsophisticated: without experience and not clever

Neither is it true that they have no demands. They do. It is just that no sane[8] person would negotiate on them.

They demand the elimination of Israel; the withdrawal of all Westerners from Muslim countries, irrespective of the wishes of people and gov-
5 ernment; the establishment of effectively Taleban states and Sharia law[9] in the Arab world en route to[10] one caliphate[11] of all Muslim nations.

We don't have to wonder what type of country those states would be. Afghanistan was such a state. Girls put out of school. Women denied
10 even rudimentary[12] rights. People living in abject[13] poverty and oppression. All of it justified by reference to[14] religious faith.

The 20th century showed how powerful political ideologies could be. This is a religious ideology, a strain[15] within the world-wide religion of Islam, as far removed from its essential decency and truth as Protestant
15 gunmen who kill Catholics or vice versa, are from Christianity. But do not let us underestimate it or dismiss[16] it.

Those who kill in its name believe genuinely that in doing it, they do God's work; they go to paradise.

"Legitimate targets"

20 From the mid 1990s onwards, statements from Al-Qaeda, gave very clear expression to this ideology: "Every Muslim, the minute he can start differentiating, carries hatred towards the Americans, Jews and Christians. This is part of our ideology. The creation of Israel is a crime and it has to be erased[17].

"You should know that targeting Americans and Jews and killing them
25 anywhere you find them on the earth is one of the greatest duties and one of the best acts of piety[18] you can offer to God Almighty."

---

8 sane: having a healthy mind
9 Sharia law: system of Islamic laws
10 en route to: on the way to
11 caliphate (Arabic): an Islamic state under an Islamic ruler
12 rudimentary: basic
13 abject: miserable
14 reference to: referring to, showing a relationship to
15 strain: kind, sort
16 to dismiss: to stop considering s.th.
17 to erase: to remove
18 piety: showing deep religious respect

Just as great is their hatred for so-called apostate[19] governments in Muslim countries. This is why mainstream Muslims are also regarded as legitimate targets.

At last year's (Labour) party conference, I talked about this ideology in these terms. 5

Its roots are not superficial, but deep, in the madrassas[20] of Pakistan, in the extreme forms of Wahabi[21] doctrine in Saudi Arabia, in the former training camps of Al-Qaeda in Afghanistan; in the cauldron[22] of Chechnya; in parts of the politics of most countries of the Middle East and many in Asia; in the extremist minority that now in every European 10 city preach hatred of the West and our way of life.

This is what we are up against. It cannot be beaten except by confronting it, symptoms and causes, head-on. Without compromise and without delusion[23].

The extremist propaganda is cleverly aimed at their target audience. It 15 plays on our tolerance and good nature.

It exploits[24] the tendency of the developed world to feel guilty, as if it is our behaviour that should change, that if we only tried to work out and act on their grievances[25], we could lift this evil, that if we changed our behaviour, they would change theirs. This is a misunderstanding of 20 a catastrophic order.

Their cause is not founded on an injustice. It is founded on a belief, one whose fanaticism is such it can't be moderated. It can't be remedied[26]. It has to be stood up to.

And, of course, they will use any issue that is a matter of dissent within 25 our democracy. But we should lay bare[27] the almost-devilish logic behind such manipulation.

---

[19] apostate: having rejected a religion
[20] madrassa (Arabic): school
[21] Wahabi: a very conservative Islamic sect
[22] cauldron ['kɔːldrn] (fig.): large pot for boiling food
[23] delusion: false beliefs about a situation
[24] to exploit: to use for your own profit or gain
[25] grievance: complaint, feeling of resentment
[26] to remedy: to correct or improve
[27] to lay bare: to show what has been covered

"Callous[28] indifference"

If it is the plight[29] of the Palestinians that drives them, why, every time it looks as if Israel and Palestine are making progress, does the same ideology perpetrate[30] an outrage[31] that turns hope back into despair?

5   If it is Afghanistan that motivates them, why blow up innocent Afghans on their way to their first ever election? If it is Iraq that motivates them, why is the same ideology killing Iraqis by terror in defiance of[32] an elected Iraqi government?

What was September 11, 2001 the reprisal[33] for? Why even after the 10 first Madrid bomb (in March 2004) and the election of a new Spanish government, were they planning another atrocity[34] when caught? Why if it is the cause of Muslims that concerns them, do they kill so many with such callous indifference?

We must pull this up by its roots. Within Britain, we must join up 15 with our Muslims community to take on the extremists. Worldwide, we should confront it everywhere it exists.

Next week I and other party leaders will meet key members of the Muslim community. Out of it I hope we can get agreed action to take this common fight forward. I want also to work with other nations to 20 promote[35] the true face of Islam worldwide.

Round the world, there are conferences already being held, numerous inter-faith dialogues in place, but we need to bring all of these activities together and give them focus.

Defeating the threat

25 We must be clear about how we win this struggle. We should take what security measures we can. But let us not kid[36] ourselves.

In the end, it is by the power of argument, debate, true religious faith and true legitimate politics that we will defeat this threat.

---

[28] callous: unfeeling
[29] plight: extreme hardship
[30] to perpetrate: to carry out
[31] outrage: cruel act
[32] in defiance of: openingly refusing to accept s.th.
[33] reprisal: a violent or aggressive act towards s.o. because of s.th. bad that this person has done to you
[34] atrocity: extremely cruel and violent act
[35] to promote: to help to develop
[36] to kid: to fool

That means not just arguing against their terrorism, but their politics and their perversion of religious faith. It means exposing[37] as the rubbish it is, the propaganda about America and its allies wanting to punish Muslims or eradicate[38] Islam.

It means championing[39] our values of freedom, tolerance and respect ⁵ for others. It means explaining why the suppression of women and the disdain[40] for democracy are wrong.

The idea that elected governments are the preserve[41] of those of any other faith or culture [other than Islam] is insulting and wrong. Muslims believe in democracy just as much as any other faith and, given the ¹⁰ chance, show it.

We must step up the urgency[42] of our efforts. Here and abroad, the times the terrorists have succeeded are all too well known.

Less known are the times they have been foiled[43]. The human life destroyed we can see. The billions of dollars every nation now spends is ¹⁵ huge and growing. And they kill without limit.

They murdered over 50 innocent people (in London) last week. But it could have been over 500. And had it been, they would have rejoiced[44].

The spirit of our age is one in which the prejudices of the past are put behind us, where our diversity is our strength. It is this which is un- ²⁰ der attack. Moderates are not moderate through weakness but through strength. Now is the time to show it in defence of our common values.

---

[37] to expose: to reveal, to bring to light, to show what was hidden
[38] to eradicate: to completely destroy
[39] to champion: to fight for or speak in support of s.th.
[40] disdain [dɪsˈdeɪn]: contempt *(Verachtung)*
[41] preserve: special area
[42] urgency: the necessity of speedy action
[43] to foil: to stop from happening
[44] to rejoice: to express great happiness about s.th.

Prime Minister David Cameron's Speech at the Munich Security Conference

5 February 2011

[...] the biggest threat that we face comes from terrorist attacks, some
5 of which are, sadly, carried out by our own citizens. It is important
to stress that terrorism is not linked exclusively to any one religion
or ethnic group. My country, the United Kingdom, still faces threats
from dissident republicans in Northern Ireland. Anarchist attacks have
occurred recently in Greece and in Italy, and of course, yourselves in
10 Germany were long scarred[1] by terrorism from the Red Army Faction[2].
Nevertheless, we should acknowledge that this threat comes in Europe
overwhelmingly from young men who follow a completely perverse,
warped[3] interpretation of Islam, and who are prepared to blow themselves up and kill their fellow citizens. [...]

15   We have got to get to the root[4] of the problem, and we need to be absolutely clear on where the origins of these terrorist attacks lie. That is
the existence of an ideology, Islamist extremism. We should be equally
clear what we mean by this term[5], and we must distinguish[6] it from
Islam. Islam is a religion observed peacefully and devoutly[7] by over a
20 billion people. Islamist extremism is a political ideology supported by
a minority. At the furthest end are those who back terrorism to promote their ultimate goal: an entire Islamist realm[8], governed by an interpretation of Sharia[9]. Move along the spectrum, and you find people
who may reject violence, but who accept various parts of the extremist
25 worldview, including real hostility[10] towards Western democracy and
liberal values. It is vital that we make this distinction[11] between religion
on the one hand, and political ideology on the other. Time and again,

---

[1] to scar: to leave s.o. with a feeling of mental pain
[2] Red Army Faction: German left wing terror group especially active in the 1970s
[3] warped: twisted
[4] root: primary source, origin
[5] term: expression
[6] to distinguish: to differentiate
[7] devoutly: in a deeply religious way
[8] realm: world
[9] Sharia (Arabic): Islamic law
[10] hostility: strong and angry opposition
[11] distinction: difference

people equate the two. They think whether someone is an extremist is dependent on how much they observe their religion. So, they talk about moderate Muslims as if all devout[12] Muslims must be extremist. This is profoundly wrong. Someone can be a devout Muslim and not be an extremist. We need to be clear: Islamist extremism and Islam are not the same thing.

This highlights[13], I think, a significant problem when discussing the terrorist threat that we face. There is so much muddled[14] thinking about this whole issue. On the one hand, those on the hard right ignore this distinction between Islam and Islamist extremism, and just say that Islam and the West are irreconcilable[15] – that there is a clash of civilisations. So, it follows: we should cut ourselves off from this religion, whether that is through forced repatriation[16], favoured by some fascists, or the banning of new mosques, as is suggested in some parts of Europe. These people fuel[17] Islamophobia, and I completely reject their argument. If they want an example of how Western values and Islam can be entirely compatible, they should look at what's happened in the past few weeks on the streets of Tunis and Cairo: hundreds of thousands of people demanding the universal right to free elections and democracy.

The point is this: the ideology of extremism is the problem; Islam emphatically[18] is not. Picking a fight with the latter will do nothing to help us to confront the former. On the other hand, there are those on the soft left who also ignore this distinction. They lump all Muslims together[19], compiling a list of grievances[20], and argue that if only governments addressed these grievances, the terrorism would stop. So, they point to the poverty that so many Muslims live in and say, "Get rid of this injustice and the terrorism will end." But this ignores the fact that many of those found guilty of terrorist offences[21] in the UK and elsewhere have been graduates[22] and often middle class. They point to grievances about

---

[12] devout: deeply religious
[13] to highlight: *hervorheben*
[14] muddled: confused
[15] irreconcilable: with no possibility of a compromise or an agreement
[16] repatriation: returning to the country of origin
[17] to fuel: to inflame, to incite *(schüren)*
[18] emphatically: definitely
[19] to lump together: to put various things together in one mass
[20] grievance: complaint about s.th. you think is unjust or unfair
[21] offence: crime
[22] graduate: a person with a university degree

Western foreign policy and say, "Stop riding roughshod over[23] Muslim countries and the terrorism will end." But there are many people, Muslim and non-Muslim alike, who are angry about Western foreign policy, but who don't resort to[24] acts of terrorism. They also point to the profusion[25]
5 of unelected leaders across the Middle East and say, "Stop propping these people up[26] and you will stop creating the conditions for extremism to flourish." But this raises the question: if it's the lack of democracy that is the problem, why are there so many extremists in free and open societies?
10 Now, I'm not saying that these issues of poverty and grievance about foreign policy are not important. Yes, of course we must tackle[27] them. Of course we must tackle poverty. Yes, we must resolve[28] the sources of tension, not least in Palestine, and yes, we should be on the side of openness and political reform in the Middle East. On Egypt, our position
15 should be clear. We want to see the transition to a more broadly-based government, with the proper building blocks of a free and democratic society. I simply don't accept that there is somehow a dead end[29] choice between a security state[30] on the one hand, and an Islamist one on the other. But let us not fool ourselves. These are just contributory factors.
20 Even if we sorted out all of the problems that I have mentioned, there would still be this terrorism. I believe the root lies in the existence of this extremist ideology. I would argue an important reason so many young Muslims are drawn to it comes down to a question of identity.

What I am about to say is drawn from the British experience, but I be-
25 lieve there are general lessons for us all. In the UK, some young men find it hard to identify with the traditional Islam practiced at home by their parents, whose customs can seem staid[31] when transplanted to modern Western countries. But these young men also find it hard to identify with Britain too, because we have allowed the weakening of our collective
30 identity. Under the doctrine of state multiculturalism, we have encouraged different cultures to live separate lives, apart from each other and

---

[23] to ride roughshod over: to treat s.o. badly without considering this person's feelings
[24] to resort to: to make use of s.th. that is bad because there is no alternative
[25] profusion: large quantity
[26] to prop up: to support
[27] to tackle: to deal with
[28] to resolve: to find a solution for s.th.
[29] dead end: *Sackgasse*
[30] security state: authoritarian state with a strong security apparatus
[31] staid [steɪd]: boring, old-fashioned

apart from the mainstream. We've failed to provide a vision of society to which they feel they want to belong. We've even tolerated these segregated communities behaving in ways that run completely counter to our values.

So, when a white person holds objectionable views, racist views for instance, we rightly condemn them. But when equally unacceptable views or practices come from someone who isn't white, we've been too cautious frankly – frankly, even fearful – to stand up to them. The failure, for instance, of some to confront the horrors of forced marriage, the practice where some young girls are bullied and sometimes taken abroad to marry someone when they don't want to, is a case in point. This hands-off tolerance has only served to reinforce[32] the sense that not enough is shared. And this all leaves some young Muslims feeling rootless. And the search for something to belong to and something to believe in can lead them to this extremist ideology. Now for sure, they don't turn into terrorists overnight, but what we see – and what we see in so many European countries – is a process of radicalisation.

Internet chatrooms are virtual meeting places where attitudes are shared, strengthened and validated[33]. In some mosques, preachers of hate can sow[34] misinformation about the plight of Muslims elsewhere. In our communities, groups and organisations led by young, dynamic leaders promote separatism by encouraging Muslims to define themselves solely in terms of their religion. All these interactions can engender[35] a sense of community, a substitute for what the wider society has failed to supply. Now, you might say, as long as they're not hurting anyone, what is the problem with all this?

Well, I'll tell you why. As evidence emerges[36] about the backgrounds of those convicted[37] of terrorist offences, it is clear that many of them were initially influenced by what some have called "non-violent extremists," and they then took those radical beliefs to the next level by embracing[38] violence. And I say this is an indictment[39] of our approach to these issues in the past. And if we are to defeat this threat, I believe it is time to turn the page on the failed policies of the past. So first, instead of ignoring this

---

[32] to reinforce: to strengthen
[33] to validate: to confirm
[34] to sow [səʊ], sowed, sown: (here): to spread
[35] to engender: to bring about, to produce
[36] to emerge: to appear after being hidden
[37] convicted: found guilty and sentenced in a court of law
[38] to embrace: to take up, to adopt
[39] indictment [ɪnˈdaɪtmənt]: (here): a sign that s.th. is very wrong

extremist ideology, we – as governments and as societies – have got to confront it, in all its forms. And second, instead of encouraging people to live apart, we need a clear sense of shared national identity that is open to everyone.

5   Let me briefly take each in turn. First, confronting and undermining this ideology. Whether they are violent in their means or not, we must make it impossible for the extremists to succeed. Now, for governments, there are some obvious ways we can do this. We must ban preachers of hate from coming to our countries. We must also proscribe[40]
10 organisations that incite terrorism against people at home and abroad. Governments must also be shrewder[41] in dealing with those that, while not violent, are in some cases part of the problem. We need to think much harder about who it's in the public interest to work with. Some organisations that seek to present themselves as a gateway[42] to the Muslim
15 community are showered with public money despite doing little to combat extremism. As others have observed, this is like turning to a right-wing fascist party to fight a violent white supremacist movement. So we should properly judge these organisations: do they believe in universal human rights – including for women and people of other faiths[43]? Do
20 they believe in equality of all before the law? Do they believe in democracy and the right of people to elect their own government? Do they encourage integration or separation? These are the sorts of questions we need to ask. Fail these tests and the presumption[44] should be not to engage with[45] organisations – so, no public money, no sharing of plat-
25 forms[46] with ministers at home.

At the same time, we must stop these groups from reaching people in publicly-funded institutions like universities or even, in the British case, prisons. Now, some say, this is not compatible with free speech and intellectual inquiry[47]. Well, I say, would you take the same view if these were
30 right-wing extremists recruiting on our campuses? Would you advocate inaction if Christian fundamentalists who believed that Muslims are the enemy were leading prayer groups in our prisons? And to those who say

---

[40] to proscribe: to ban, to forbid
[41] shrewd: clever
[42] gateway: s.th. that provides a link
[43] faith [feɪθ]: religion
[44] presumption: *Annahme*
[45] to engage with: to work with
[46] platform: a place to express views publicly
[47] inquiry: act of asking questions

these non-violent extremists are actually helping to keep young, vulner-able[48] men away from violence, I say nonsense.

Would you allow the far right groups a share of public funds if they promise to help you lure[49] young white men away from fascist terrorism? Of course not. But, at root, challenging this ideology means exposing its ideas for what they are, and that [it] is completely unjustifiable. We need to argue that terrorism is wrong in all circumstances. We need to argue that prophecies of a global war of religion pitting[50] Muslims against the rest of the world are nonsense.

Now, governments cannot do this alone. The extremism we face is a distortion[51] of Islam, so these arguments, in part, must be made by those within Islam. So let us give voice to those followers of Islam in our own countries – the vast, often unheard majority – who despise[52] the extrem-ists and their world view. Let us engage groups that share our aspira-tions[53].

Now, second, we must build stronger societies and stronger identities at home. Frankly, we need a lot less of the passive tolerance of recent years and a much more active, muscular liberalism. A passively toler-ant society says to its citizens, as long as you obey the law we will just leave you alone. It stands neutral between different values. But I believe a genuinely liberal country does much more; it believes in certain values and actively promotes them. Freedom of speech, freedom of worship, democracy, the rule of law, equal rights regardless of race, sex or sexual-ity. It says to its citizens, this is what defines us as a society: to belong here is to believe in these things. Now, each of us in our own countries, I believe, must be unambiguous[54] and hard-nosed[55] about this defence of our liberty.

There are practical things that we can do as well. That includes making sure that immigrants speak the language of their new home and ensuring that people are educated in the elements of a common culture and cur-riculum. Back home, we're introducing National Citizen Service: a two-month programme for sixteen-year-olds from different backgrounds to live and work together. I also believe we should encourage meaningful

---

[48] vulnerable ['vʌlnərəbl]: easily influenced
[49] to lure: to tempt, to attract with the promise of a reward
[50] to pit: to place in a competition or fight to see who is the stronger
[51] distortion: perversion
[52] to despise: to strongly dislike
[53] aspiration: strong desire to achieve s.th.
[54] unambiguous: clearly stated and defined
[55] hard-nosed: not affected by feelings

and active participation in society, by shifting[56] the balance of power away from the state and towards the people. That way, common purpose can be formed as people come together and work together in their neighbourhoods. It will also help build stronger pride in local identity, so people feel free to say, "Yes, I am a Muslim, I am a Hindu, I am Christian, but I am also a Londoner or a Berliner, too." It's that identity, that feeling of belonging in our countries, that I believe is the key to achieving true cohesion[57].

So, let me end with this. This terrorism is completely indiscriminate[58] and has been thrust[59] upon us. It cannot be ignored or contained; we have to confront it with confidence – confront the ideology that drives it by defeating the ideas that warp[60] so many young minds at their root[61], and confront the issues of identity that sustain[62] it by standing for a much broader and generous vision of citizenship in our countries. Now, none of this will be easy. We will need stamina[63], patience and endurance[64], and it won't happen at all if we act alone. This ideology crosses not just our continent but all continents, and we are all in this together. At stake are[65] not just lives, it is our way of life. That is why this is a challenge we cannot avoid; it is one we must rise to and overcome. Thank you.

---

[56] to shift: to change the position of s.th.
[57] cohesion [kəʊˈhiːʒn]: the quality of firmly holding or sticking together
[58] indiscriminate: without careful thought, random
[59] thrust: forced
[60] to warp: to distort, to pervert
[61] root: origin
[62] to sustain [səˈsteɪn]: to uphold, to support
[63] stamina: physical and mental strength that lasts for a long time
[64] endurance: ability to deal with a difficult situation for a long period of time
[65] to be at stake: *auf dem Spiel stehen*

A History of Burnings and Bannings
A Selected List

c. 411 BC Aristophanes' play *Lysistrata* was condemned by Plutarch. *Lysistrata* was also banned by the Nazis during the Nazi occupation of Greece in 1942 and again by the military *junta* in 1967; as well as the US customs and mails between 1867 and 1930.   5

c. 1 BC Ovid's **The Art of Love** and other work earned him his exile in 8 BC. In Florence in 1497, Savonarola burned his works for being erotic, against religion, and tending to corrupt. In 1599, the Archbishop of Canterbury condemned Ovid's *Elegies* in translation to the flames, 10 for "immorality." US customs banned the import of **The Art of Love** in 1929.

12th – 17th centuries **The Talmud**, the main source of rabbinical teaching, disputations and Jewish lore[1], was burned, banned, and confiscated repeatedly by the Catholic Church in various parts of Europe.   15

1409 **The Bible** in translation was banned by the Synod of Canterbury. In 1525, the New Testament, translated by William Tyndale, the first printed book in England, was banned. He was imprisoned, then burned at the stake along with copies of his Bible in 1536. In 1624, Luther's Bible was condemned in Germany by papal authority.   20

1542 **The Koran** was seized and confiscated by Protestant authorities in Basel, then released at Martin Luther's intervention.

1633 Galileo's **Dialogue on the Two Great World Systems** was banned by Pope Urban VIII. Some of Galileo's other works were burned.

1644 Milton's **Areopagitica** was condemned by Oliver Cromwell for its 25 advocacy[2] of freedom of the press.

1649 Roger Bacon's entire works were banned by the Spanish Inquisition.

1664 Under Louis XIV Moliere's *Tartuffe* was banned from public (though not court) performance.

---

[1] lore: stories and traditions
[2] advocacy: public support

1720 Daniel Defoe's **Robinson Crusoe** was placed on the papal index[3] as forbidden reading.

1734 John Locke's *An Essay Concerning Human Understanding* (French translation) was placed on the papal index as forbidden reading

5 1792 Thomas Paine's **The Rights of Man** and other works (also banned in England) were placed on the papal index as forbidden reading.

1827 Immanuel Kant's **Critique of Pure Reason** (Italian translation) was placed on the papal index as forbidden reading.

1834 Victor Hugo's **Notre-Dame de Paris**, and in 1864 **Les Miserables**
10 were placed on the papal index as forbidden reading.

1836 Heinrich Heine's various works were placed on the papal index as forbidden reading.

1841 Honoré Balzac's **Contes drolatiques** and other works were placed on the papal index as forbidden reading.

15 1863 Alexandre Dumas' love stories, including **La Dame aux camélias** were placed on the papal index as forbidden reading.

1856 Gustave Flaubert was prosecuted[4] for **Madame Bovary**.

1859 Charles Darwin's **On the Origin of Species** was refused by Cambridge University Library.

20 1912 James Joyce's **Dubliners** was suppressed in Ireland and elsewhere.

1928 D. H. Lawrence had the first edition of **Lady Chatterley's Lover** privately printed in Florence; it was seized by British customs. Not until 1960 did the book finally find a publisher, Penguin. Penguin fought the obscenity trial which followed in November. The book was also banned
25 in Australia and the United States.

1929–53 In the Soviet Union under Joseph Stalin, a great number of writers were censored, tortured, murdered, exiled, amongst them Babel, Osip and Nadezhda Mandelstam, Boris Pasternak, Akhmatova, Zoshchenko and Solzhenitsyn.

30 1933 On 10 May, only a few months after seizing power, the Nazis organised book burnings in Germany's major cities in an attempt to "purify" the

---

[3] index: list
[4] to prosecute: to officially charge s.o. with a crime and bring to court

nation of "degenerate" ideas. In Berlin on the Opernplatz, some twenty thousand books from libraries and bookshops were thrown onto a bonfire[5], while chanting[6] about the purification of German literature and thought. Many of the authors were Jewish – Heinrich Heine, Hermann Kesten, Karl Marx, Sigmund Freud, Albert Einstein, Franz Kafka, or such as Thomas Mann, married to Jews; others were simply considered degenerate such as Hemingway, Jack London, and Upton Sinclair.

1948 Several of the American writer, William Faulkner's novels were banned in Philadelphia.

1959 Naguib Mahfouz, the great Egyptian Nobel Prize-winning author of **Children of Gebelawi**, earned a *fatwa* for apostasy[7] from Omar Abdul Rahman. Many of the novelist's works have been banned in the Middle East. In 1994, thirty-five years after the *fatwa* was issued[8], Mahfouz, at the age of eighty-three, was stabbed[9] in the neck by two extremists outside his Cairo home.

1988 Sir Salman Rushdie's **The Satanic Verses** was banned in India on 5 October, ten days after its UK publication. It was then banned in South Africa.

1989 On 14 January, **The Satanic Verses** was burned in Bradford. Muslim protests also took place in Hyde Park, London.

1989–99 On 14 February 1989 Iran's Ayatollah Khomeini proclaimed a *fatwa* against Sir Salman Rushdie and his publisher, Penguin. A price was put on his life, whereupon the writer went into hiding. There were bannings of the book and protests in India, Turkey and elsewhere. The Japanese translator of the book was killed. A special paperback edition of the book came out published – in solidarity with Penguin and the author – by a group of publishers.

1993 Taslima Nasrin, the Bengali novelist, poet, journalist and doctor, had a *fatwa* declared against her in Bangladesh for the novel **Shame**, which described the plight[10] of a Hindu family under attack by Muslim fundamentalists.

---

[5] bonfire: large, outdoor fire
[6] to chant: to shout or sing the same phrase repeatedly
[7] apostasy: rejection of accepted religious beliefs
[8] to issue: to make known publicly, to proclaim
[9] to stab: to push a knife into a person's body
[10] plight: sad and miserable life

1995 Mark Twain's **Huckleberry Finn,** because of not being politically correct according to some African Americans, was removed from classes in various US schools.

2001 The Harry Potter books were burned on a bonfire in New Mexico, USA by people accusing the fictional boy wizard of being the devil. Horror books by Stephen King were also burned.

2004 Theo van Gogh, Dutch film-maker, was murdered for his film *Submission* by Mohammed Bouyeri, who left a letter with *jihadist*[11] slogans on his body. Somalian-born Dutch politician Ayaan Hirsi Ali, who wrote the script for *Submission,* went into hiding after threats and has been living under police protection. In 2005 a court in The Hague rejected a petition from a Muslim group to bar Ayaan Hirsi Ali from making another film about the treatment of women under Islam.

2006 March, Damascus, Syria – To express their displeasure at a series of Muhammad caricatures printed originally in the major Danish daily *Jyllands-Posten* thousands of protesters gathered for a peaceful protest outside the Danish Embassy in the early afternoon, but it quickly escalated. Demonstrators began throwing stones, broke through a police barricade and stormed the embassy. Shortly afterward, they set fire to the building. "With our blood and souls we defend you, O Prophet of God," a number of them chanted. Demonstrators replaced the Danish flag with a green flag reading: "There is no god but God and Muhammad is the messenger of God."

2011 Terry Jones, pastor of a small Protestant sect known for its anti-Islam activities, publically burned a copy of **The Koran** in Gainesville, Florida on March 20. There was a reaction by a Muslim mob in Afghanistan at the beginning of April 2011. Many people were killed.

---

[11] jihadist (Arabic): having to do with a holy war to defend Islam

Some Quotes about Censorship and Burning Books

"There are worse crimes than burning books. One of them is not reading them."
– Joseph Alexandrovitch Brodsky, 1991, Russian-American poet, born
St. Petersburg and exiled 1972 (1940–1996)

"Everyone is in favor of free speech. Hardly a day passes without its being extolled[1], but some people's idea of it is that they are free to say what they like, but if anyone else says anything back, that is an outrage[2]."
– Winston Churchill

"You see these dictators on their pedestals, surrounded by the bayonets of their soldiers and the truncheons[3] of their police. Yet in their hearts there is unspoken – unspeakable! – fear. They are afraid of words and thoughts! Words spoken abroad, thoughts stirring[4] at home, all the more powerful because they are forbidden. These terrify them. A little mouse – a little tiny mouse! – of thought appears in the room, and even the mightiest potentates[5] are thrown into panic."
– Winston Churchill

"Don't join the book burners. Don't think you are going to conceal[6] thoughts by concealing evidence that they ever existed."
– Dwight D. Eisenhower, speech at Dartmouth College, June 14, 1953

"Every burned book enlightens[7] the world."
– Ralph Waldo Emerson (1803–1882)

"They that can give up essential liberty to obtain a little temporary safety deserve neither liberty nor safety."
– Benjamin Franklin, Historical Review of Pennsylvania, 1759

---

[1] to extol: to praise
[2] outrage: scandal
[3] truncheon ['trʌntʃn]: short, thick stick used by the police
[4] to stir: to begin to come into existence
[5] potentate: powerful ruler
[6] to conceal: to hide
[7] to enlighten: to give more information

"If all printers were determined not to print anything till they were sure it would offend[8] nobody, there would be very little printed."
– Benjamin Franklin, 1730

"Books won't stay banned. They won't burn. Ideas won't go to jail. In the long run of history, the censor and the inquisitor have always lost. The only sure weapon against bad ideas is better ideas. The source of better ideas is wisdom. The surest path to wisdom is a liberal education."
– Alfred Whitney Griswold (1906–1963), President of Yale, *Essays on Education*

"Where they have burned books, they will end in burning human beings."
– Heinrich Heine

"The sooner we all learn to make a decision between disapproval[9] and censorship, the better off society will be … Censorship cannot get at the real evil, and it is an evil in itself."
– Granville Hicks (1901–1982), American literary critic

"Children deprived of[10] words become school dropouts; dropouts deprived of hope behave delinquently[11]. Amateur censors blame delinquency on reading immoral books and magazines, when in fact, the inability to read anything is the basic trouble."
– Peter S. Jennison

"Books and ideas are the most effective weapons against intolerance and ignorance."
– Lyndon Baines Johnson, February 11, 1964

---

[8] to offend: to insult
[9] disapproval: considering s.th. bad or wrong
[10] to deprive of: to prevent s.o. from having s.th. important
[11] delinquently: against the law

"We are not afraid to entrust[12] the American people with unpleasant facts, foreign ideas, alien[13] philosophies, and competitive values. For a nation that is afraid to let its people judge the truth and falsehood in an open market is a nation that is afraid of its people."
– John F. Kennedy   5

"The burning of an author's books, imprisonment for an opinion's sake, has always been the tribute that an ignorant age pays to the genius of its time."
– Joseph Lewis, **Voltaire: The Incomparable Infidel**, 1929

"One cannot and must not try to erase the past merely because it does 10
not fit the present."
– Golda Meir, Israeli political leader (1898 – 1978)

"Censorship of anything, at any time, in any place, on whatever pretense[14], has always been and always be the last resort[15] of the boob[16] and the bigot."
– Eugene Gladstone O'Neill, American playwright (1888 – 1953)   15

"All of us can think of a book … that we hope none of our children or any other children have taken off the shelf. But if I have the right to re-move that book from the shelf – and that work I abhor[17] – then you also have exactly the same right and so does everyone else. And then we have no books left on the shelf for any of us."   20
– Katherine Paterson, American author of children's books (1932–)

"Free societies … are societies in motion, and with motion comes ten-sion, dissent, friction. Free people strike sparks, and those sparks are the best evidence of freedom's existence."
– Sir Salman Rushdie   25

"What is freedom of expression? Without the freedom to offend, it ceas-es to exist."
– Sir Salman Rushdie

---

[12] to entrust: to put into the care of s.o.
[13] alien: foreign
[14] pretense: excuse
[15] resort: course of action
[16] boob: stupid person
[17] to abhor: to hate

"Censorship ends in logical completeness when nobody is allowed to read any books except the books that nobody reads."
– George Bernard Shaw, Irish playwright and critic (1856–1950)

"All censorships exist to prevent anyone from challenging current conceptions and existing institutions. All progress is initiated[18] by challenging current conceptions, and executed[19] by supplanting[20] existing institutions. Consequently the first condition of progress is the removal of censorship."
– George Bernard Shaw, Preface to *Mrs. Warren's Profession*

"Censorship reflects a society's lack of confidence in itself. It is the hallmark[21] of an authoritarian regime ..."
– Justice Potter Stewart, dissenting Ginzberg v. United States, 383 U.S. 463 (1966)

"Once a government is committed to the principle of[22] silencing the voice of opposition, it has only one way to go, and that is down the path of increasingly repressive measures, until it becomes a source of terror to all its citizens and creates a country where everyone lives in fear."
– Harry S. Truman, message to Congress, August 8, 1950

"All these people talk so eloquently about getting back to good old-fashioned values. Well, as an old poop[23] I can remember back to when we had those old-fashioned values, and I say let's get back to the good old-fashioned First Amendment of the good old-fashioned Constitution of the United States – and to hell with the censors! Give me knowledge or give me death!"
– Kurt Vonnegut, author

"The dirtiest book of all is the expurgated[24] book."
– Walt Whitman, American poet

---

[18] to initiate: to set in motion
[19] to execute: to carry out
[20] to supplant: to replace
[21] hallmark: typical characteristic
[22] is committed to the principle of: has decided on the policy of
[23] poop (slang): fellow
[24] expurgated: with offensive parts removed

"There is no such thing as a moral book or an immoral book. Books are well written or badly written. That is all."
– Oscar Wilde, **The Picture of Dorian Gray**, 1891

"The books that the world calls immoral are the books that show the world its own shame." 5
– Oscar Wilde, **The Picture of Dorian Gray**, 1891

"An idea that is not dangerous is unworthy of being called an idea at all."
– Oscar Wilde

"If liberty means anything at all it means the right to tell people what 10 they do not want to hear."
– George Orwell in an unpublished preface to **Animal Farm**

"Everyone has the right to freedom of opinion and expression: the right includes freedom to hold opinions without interference, to seek, receive and impart[25] information and ideas through any media regardless of 15 frontiers."
– Universal Declaration of Human Rights

"To criticise a person for their race is manifestly[26] irrational and ridiculous but to criticise their religion, that is a right. That is a freedom … The freedom to criticise ideas, any ideas – even if they are sincerely held 20 beliefs – is one of the fundamental freedoms of society and a law which attempts to say you can criticise and ridicule ideas as long as they are not religious ideas is a very peculiar law indeed."
– Rowan Atkinson (1955–   ), British comedian

---

[25] to impart: to pass on
[26] manifestly: obviously

[...] Multicultural ideologues emphasize the harm that uncensored speech is believed to do to defenseless individuals. Unquestionably, slurs[27] and insults can be injurious, but is the injury words inflict on[28] sensibilities sufficiently weighty[29] and enduring[30] to justify so drastic a remedy[31] as
5 limitations on free speech?

[...] Ray Bradbury foresaw all this more than forty years ago in **Fahrenheit 451** – the demand of minorities to burn the books that might make them unhappy. "Colored people don't like **Little Black Sambo**. Burn it. White people don't feel good about **Uncle Tom's Cabin**. Burn it.
10 ... Don't step on the toes of the dog lovers, cat lovers, doctors, lawyers, merchants, chiefs, Mormons, Baptists, Unitarians, second-generation Chinese, Swedes, Italians, Germans, Texans, Brooklynites, Irish men, people from Oregon or Mexico."

If we start down the insensitivity road, we will end up endorsing[32] Ayatollah Khomeini[33] and his crusade against **The Satanic Verses**. Does
15 the fact that **The Satanic Verses** hurts the feelings of devout[34] Muslims really justify the murder of Sir Salman Rushdie?
– from "Multiculturalism versus The Bill of Rights" by Arthur Schlesinger, Jr. first presented as the Frank M. Coffin Lecture given at the University of Maine Law School in 1994

---

[27] slur: an unfair remark about s.o. that may cause other people to think badly of this person
[28] to inflict on s.o./s.th.: *zufügen*
[29] sufficiently weighty: important and serious enough
[30] enduring: lasting for a long time
[31] remedy: way of dealing with or improving an unpleasant or difficult situation, solution
[32] to endorse: to express formal support or approval for s.o. or s.th.
[33] Ayatollah Khomeini (1902–1989): ruler of Iran after the overthrow of the Shah in 1979 — In early 1989 he called on all Muslims to kill Sir Salman Rushdie because of the supposed blasphemy against Muhammad in his novel **The Satanic Verses**.
[34] devout [di'vaʊt]: deeply religious

An Interview with Hanif Kureishi

Posted on 26 April 2010

Hanif Kureishi is one of the most popular and acclaimed[1] British writers today. His first play was produced at the Royal Court theatre when
he was 22. He reached a new level of eminence[2] when his screenplay for   5
My Beautiful Laundrette was nominated for an Academy Award and
his novel *The Buddha of Suburbia* won a Whitbread First Novel Award.
Since then he has written many critically acclaimed novels, short stories and screenplays including *Intimacy* (1998), *The Mother* (2003) and
Something to Tell You (2008). In 2007 he was awarded a CBE[3] in rec-   10
ognition for his services to literature and drama. Last month saw the
publication of his *Collected Short Stories.*

Interview by Catherine Fildes

*Have you been writing this morning?, I ask Kureishi as we sit down to the
shrill French music playing in the background of his regular haunt[4] – for*   15
*interviews at least – Café Rouge. Yes – well – I've done a lot of fucking
about, he replies. Our conversation is not lively at the start: he's had his
head in the essays of his students on the Creative Writing MA[5] at Kingston
University, and I've been nervously flipping through the 600 page-plus
volume of his recently-published* **Collected Short Stories.** *He's curt[6] and*   20
*I'm shy. Nonetheless we proceed and in the next hour cover topics from
David Cameron to how writing can feel like a "waste of time" …*

**The Literateur: When I was reading some of your essays about how
to discipline yourself to write, I found it quite similar to the way I
have to discipline myself to do a PhD.**   25

Hanif Kureishi: Well there are resistances aren't there? Eventually you
  have to get on with it. Once you get on with it, it's fun – I like the idea
  of it rather than the actual work though. When I have an idea for a sto-

---

[1] acclaimed: acknowledged for excellence
[2] eminence: distinction, fame
[3] CBE: Commander of the Order of the British Empire
[4] haunt: a place you frequently go to
[5] MA: Magister Artium, an academic degree
[6] curt: abrupt, using few words

ry I find it much more exciting to have the idea than to have to write it down. Once I've had the idea, writing it down's pretty boring.

TL: **What about editing?**

HK: That's even worse.

5 TL: **I wanted to ask about my own PhD topic, which is on "British Muslim" literature – a very fashionable topic at the moment ...**

HK: Is it?

TL: **Well, you must know ...**

HK: I don't know very much about Muslims. I'm sure you know more

10 about them than I do. I've written about some of the things that I heard about. A writer can steal stories from anyone, from anywhere.

TL: **Yet I know you conducted research within the British Muslim community for *The Black Album*, visiting mosques and sitting with young Muslims whilst they were listening to the Friday *khutba*[7].**

15 **Do you think the environment for Muslims is still the same?**

HK: No, no. I mean, when I did that research, that was 1991. Obviously not: the turning point was 9/11. I think Muslims think of themselves differently. I mean, "Muslim" was really associated in 1991 with the "Rushdie affair" – that you were a Muslim meant that you were radi-

20 cal, that you saw Islam as a political ideology. Now someone would call themselves "Muslim" in the sense that they have a certain attitude to God, and to their own history or tradition or background. So, what happened since, as it were, has helped Muslims to think about who they are and where they stand ... the whole landscape is completely

25 different. Radical Islam was originally a form of liberation, like colonialism really ...

TL: **Well, the Iranian revolution was definitely associated with Marxist ideals at least – whether it fulfilled those ideals was another matter ...**

30 HK: That's right. That's a good way of putting it.

TL: **I was interested in the ideas of liberation and liberalism, and how they are both a part of Islamist ideology and Islamist reform movements, but then get distorted[8]. I was re-reading *The Black Album*, which is really fascinating for my own research. At points in the**

35 **novel, Islam does seem to be equated with liberalism[9] from a materialist, late-capitalist culture, and at other points it is wholly opposed to it – so there are different "liberalisms" within the novel ...**

---

[7] khutba (Arabic): sermon
[8] distorted: twisted, completely changed in a negative way
[9] liberalism: i.e. being liberated from

HK: Liberalism can be a battering ram[10], or it can become a fortress: it might become a battering ram rather like Marxism itself, whereas in certain circumstances it can become a prison. You have to ask what these ideologies are being used for – that's a more interesting question to ask than "what are they in themselves?" That's how I like to look 5 at it. What is ideology for? How is it being used? Who is it being used by? And the most important question: when? Radical Islam as it was used in Iran wouldn't be the same as radical Islam in London today, and it's not the same as Islam in Leeds or Bradford today.

TL: Do you still feel angry after the Rushdie affair? A lot of writing 10 **– including *The Black Album* – was produced in response to the Muslim reaction.**

HK: Do I still feel angry? I think it was a good opportunity for us to reflect on what writing was for, what books are for. We take it for granted that books are a jolly good thing and you should say whatever 15 you want in them: now all of us have questioned our practices. What is respect? How far can you go? What can you say? What does it mean to use violent language against somebody else, etc. These are really important questions, and the Rushdie affair brought all that back, really brought it out. This was a worldwide controversy about a book, that 20 most people hadn't read, and even those who did read it were none-the-wiser. It was a fascinating time.

TL: I think it's true that people decontextualise[11] radical or extremist Islam even when they think they're speaking about something very specific: it is to do with location as much as anything and what it's 25 **reacting against. Things which seem to be liberations often turn into fundamentalisms but different fundamentalisms in different times and places. What I thought of *The Black Album* was that it was articulating something very specific about British Islam as reacting against Thatcherism. Whereas in Salman Rushdie's writ-** 30 **ings or Nadeem Aslam's[12] writings there are very different kinds of fundamentalisms being exposed[13].**

HK: I guess as a writer, I'm more interested in character than ideology. Or, I'd be interested in the way this person believes. For me, it isn't

---

[10] battering ram (fig.): a long, heavy piece of wood used in wars in the past for breaking down doors and walls

[11] to decontextualise: to examine s.th. without taking the circumstances into consideration

[12] Nadam Aslam: Pakistan born English writer

[13] to expose: to reveal, to show s.th. that has been hidden

about working out what I think, and then saying: "I believe in free speech in this way …" Rather, what's interesting is the argument, and how Islam or Marxism is used, and how it relates to someone's life, under a political context. Keeping all of that going, and showing it. So the argument is to show the argument. In the end, what one believes as a liberalist or a fundamentalist is quite banal[14]. They're all truisms ultimately based on force. It's the other stuff, the superstructure of things that I'm interested in.

TL: "My Son the Fanatic" is a short story dealing with the same issues as *The Black Album*. I wondered about the form of the short story in relation to what you are saying: are they able to represent the psychology of a single character more neatly than a novel?

HK: The story – some of them are long and some of them are short. It's not like a film. All films are between 1½ and 2 hours, so they're quite formal – but a story can be any length. So it's a more luxurious form for a writer – you start, and when the story's finished you stop.

TL: Yes, well some of the new stories in the *Collected Short Stories* are very short …

HK: They were long when I started off, but then I spent the whole of my time editing: when you get to the end you think, it took me ages to do that, is that all it is?

TL: This reminds me of Raymond Carver[15] – that kind of brutal editing – do you have an editor who will do this job for you?

HK: I wouldn't allow it. I wouldn't hand something over to somebody else. American editors are like writers. They really shorten the stuff. They're co-writers, and you don't really consider it to be your own piece in the end. I wouldn't allow it now. I'm old enough to stand up to it. But when you're thirty-one, and some editor's attacking your work, it's really hard.

TL: Has your relationship with editors and publishers then changed considerably? Do you have more bargaining[16] power nowadays?

HK: Well, I wouldn't with a film. With a film I'd be nobody: the producers and directors have a lot of power. But with a short story I can write what I like.

TL: Was it your decision to bring out the *Collected Short Stories* then?

---

[14] banal [bəˈnɑːl]: very ordinary, commonplace
[15] Raymond Carver (1938–1988): American short story writer and poet
[16] to bargain: to discuss price and conditions before coming to an agreement

HK: No, it was my editor's. Basically what you have to do, if you're a
writer, is to repackage the stuff over again, just rebrand[17] it, put it in
a different cover, and then it gets re-reviewed and so on and so on …
You're trying to sell books so that you can make a living. And also it's
getting much harder, especially for younger writers. I was lucky, my   5
career coincided[18] with a boom. In the 1980s when you were a writer
you could earn a lot of money. I really believe that's over. People are
going to start downloading stuff really cheaply. In the old days you'd
buy a hard-jacket[19] that cost £15. And now people can download stuff
onto their phones and onto the iPad for a fiver[20]. And soon they'll find   10
out, like my children do, how to download it all for free. My children
download music all the time and they never pay for it, and it never
occurs to them to go to the shops and buy a CD.

TL: You do start to wonder when the book will be completely out-
moded …   15

HK: I didn't say that. I think the book will remain moded[21]. I just don't
think people will want to pay for it. A bit like the newspapers: it's out-
rageous that the *Sunday Times* wants me to pay to read it. Why would
you pay? There's no need for it. I don't think the book is outmoded,
it's just whether people will want to pay for it. But then, it's the case   20
that my children rarely read books …

TL: Do you think that will change as they grow up?

HK: They think it's really nerdy[22]. For them it's shameful to be seen
reading a book. I do think too much importance is attributed to reading books though. But on the other hand, that's what I've wasted my   25
life doing.

TL: Do you still feel that writing is a waste of time?

HK: Well, what would you prefer to do – if I had to choose between
going for a bike ride with one of my sons, having lunch in the park,
sitting around gossiping, then going home – that's what I did with   30
them yesterday – would I rather do that or sit in my room writing a
book? I'd rather be with my sons. That seems a much more valuable
and spontaneous life to live. What I mean is that I think people often
fetishise[23] books and reading. A kid who reads is a "good" kid, i.e.

---

[17] to rebrand: to change the name of a product
[18] to coincide: to take place at the same time
[19] hard-jacket: *gebunde Ausgabe*
[20] fiver: five pounds
[21] moded: in fashion
[22] nerdy: boring, stupid, not fashionable
[23] to fetishise: to attach excessive importance to s.th.

he's not noisy; but on the other hand you're not interacting with other people, you're interacting with a dead text. So I have lots of questions about all of this, interesting questions.

TL: **I do think that the novel has been extolled[24] as a symbol of "democracy," and something which you can learn from and which will change your life. And I don't think that's true to the extent at which it's been propagated.**

HK: Yeah, but if you were living in a fascist or a communist or a radical Islamic state, which most people in this world have done, then the book would represent something very important, especially in Stalinist Russia, or in Pakistan today. The book would be a very liberating thing in that context.

TL: **The novel has been extolled in the West also ...**

HK: It is a very liberating form, because people do speak, and they speak freely as they can from their unconscious ...

TL: **Do you find that with the "bigger" forms like films and novels, that you can speak more freely, that there are multiple perspectives, or can you achieve that in an essay and short story as well?**

HK: Probably not in an essay – an essay would be written from a single point of view. But yes, if you take a film like *My Beautiful Laundrette*: when it came out it was considered to be very radical. It wasn't a big deal when it was shown in Soho, but everywhere else people were shocked by it. People came up to me and said: "I was thirteen years old when I saw that film, and afterwards I realised I was gay". A lot of people.

TL: **Do you see yourself as a spokesperson for multiculturalism?**

HK: I like hybridity[25] and I like mixing up, but I'm not a fan of multiculturalism anymore: I've become a Marxist in the last three days. I was a fan of multiculturalism when it was useful to have it, in the 1970s, and now we have it and I don't think it's very interesting. On the one hand, it's just festivals and food. And on the other hand, it's everybody being the same. The one thing that multiculturalism can't deal with is the fact that some things are not compatible with one another. Multiculturalism creates a mush[26] where everything's nice, and I think that's really oppressive.

TL: **Another criticism of "multiculturalism" was that it placed the emphasis on communities rather than individuals: whereas "cos-**

---

[24] to extol: to praise very much
[25] hybridity: the mixing of cultures
[26] mush: soft, thick mass

mopolitanism" proposed that you could pick and choose identities, that you could become individually hybrid, "multiculturalism" tends to segregate people into groups …

HK: Segregate them and make them the same though, in their blandness[27]. A bit like saying, "we're all religious." I only like religion when 5
it's really horrible, when it's hateful – only then does it have any point.
Look at what's happened with the Catholic Church – it'll soon be
so regulated that Catholicism will become really bland – there won't
be any hatred left. It'll be a bit like David Cameron[28]: there'll be no
Tory[29] hatred left, no fire in it. I mean I liked Thatcher because I hated 10
her.

**TL: I was thinking about the generational difference between us. My
generation hasn't had any experience of Thatcherism; we've grown
up in a discursively[30] "multicultural" environment where racism
isn't as big a deal as it was in the 70s and 80s. Yet a lot of your char- 15
acters have grown up in this period …**

HK: And multiculturalism grew out of that… But now I think multiculturalism's useless.

TL: So do you have any idea of what we should be moving towards?

HK: I think a class-based politics. 20

**TL: Maybe the election[31] will bring that to the fore[32] … what did you
think of the ITV[33] debate between the three party leaders?**

HK: I was pretty bored by it. I thought there should be a class war and
an attack on the bankers, and also on the government that would have
allowed this to happen – the government that is making the public re- 25
pay a debt[34] that the others have made – this seems to me to be grounds
for revolution.

**TL: Maybe we are in a more apathetic[35] age, where it's only the reli-
gious reformist movements that seem to have any angry spirit in
them.** 30

---

[27] blandness: the quality of having no distinctive qualities
[28] David Cameron: head of the Conservative Party and Prime Minister of Great Britain since 2010
[29] Tory: having to do with the Conservative Party in Great Britain
[30] discursively: involving discussions
[31] the election: the general election of May 6, 2010, which resulted in a Conservative – Liberal Democratic party coalition
[32] to bring to the fore: to make s.th. noticed
[33] ITV: a private TV station in Great Britain
[34] debt [det]: *Schuld*
[35] apathetic: showing little enthusiasm or interest

HK: I think we need a new Left, and a Left that needs to evolve – that will emerge and form new ideals – certainly focused on education, and housing, and health: it would be a radical attack on the current government.

5 **TL: You don't think the Liberal Democrats could provide that?**

HK: I'm probably going to vote Lib Dem; I'm not voting for Labour and I'm not voting for the Tories. Yet it's a shame that this is an Obama moment and we don't have anyone with radicalism or intelligence. I like Gordon Brown but I couldn't forgive him for the Iraq War and I

10 couldn't forgive him for something worse: the liberation of the bankers who have ripped off[36] the public. I don't blame the bankers – if you leave your doors unlocked you can't complain that a burglar has come into your house.

TL: A lot of critiques[37] have discussed the cosmopolitanism in your

15 **writings: the ability to pick and choose your identity. And yet at the same time, when I was reading your short stories I was really struck by the materiality of them, the fact that you can't escape the body. Are there limits to how cosmopolitan you can be?**

HK: Yes, you can't just pick up any identity: you have the parents you

20 have, you have the country, the time and the class; and you can mess around with that. To get a new identity means giving up something, and you might have to give up quite a lot – you can't just pick and choose, like buying a new coat or a new purse. It's very limited. But then identities are very limited too, and that's why I think that iden-

25 tity politics and multiculturalism are quite limited – to define people as "gay," "woman,", "Muslim,", "Jew" or whatever – these are very important labels[38] for certain times and certain circumstances. But I think in the West now, these have rather worn out their welcome[39]: you're not only gay, you might also be a parent, you use the health

30 service, you identify with other people who are unemployed. Identity is useful for some things at certain times and not for others. You do have to be flexible. On the other hand, as I say, you can't just become anybody.

---

[36] to rip off (colloquial): to cheat s.o.
[37] critique: critical study
[38] label: *Etikett*
[39] worn out their welcome (idiom): are no longer acceptable

TL: And you're moving towards an idea of identities as dialogic[40] as well – the fact that you're always articulating your identity to somebody.

HK: Yes, exactly. These things are only useful in terms of where the argument is, what it does and how it works. The place. And that's why in a story you have lots of characters to speak to each other. 5

TL: The word "important" seems to repeat itself extensively in the collection, as former ideals are revised or dropped, replaced by new desires or left blank[41]. An especially interesting transition is between the ending of "Blue, Blue, Pictures of You," where Laura admits that 10 "she had only wanted a good time" in her youth and now "wanted something important to do," and the beginning of the next story, "My Son the Fanatic," where Ali turns to Islamism in defiance[42] against his upbringing because "there are more important things to be done" in life. Would you agree that your stories are about the 15 longing for, if not the realisation of, the "important?"

HK: These are real questions – the relation between hedonism[43] and meaning, or between being selfish and being good. The value of what you do. Freud doesn't talk about this but Jung[44] writes about it a lot. When I'm looking after my son I don't question what I'm doing – I'm 20 just looking after this boy because it's a good thing to do and it makes me a good father. If I'm writing a story, I may think: "do I need to write a story or shall I go down to the pub?" These are questions that we have; it's easy to drive out meaning. Meaning is often tenuous[45] – you can create meaninglessness by the stupidity of the questions. The right way to live is something you work out for yourself all the time. 25

posted on 26 April 2010: http://www.literateur.com/an-interview-with-hanif-kureishi/
reprinted with the kind permission of the interviewer, Catherine Fildes, and the editor of *The Literateur,* Kit Toda

---

[40] dialogic: involving discussions with another person
[41] blank: with no content, empty
[42] in defiance: open refusal to obey s.th., open resistance, opposition
[43] hedonism: being only interested in pleasure
[44] Carl Gustav Jung (1875–1961): Swiss psychologist who broke with Freud on the issue of the importance of the sex instinct
[45] tenuous: weak and uncertain in a way that s.th. may no longer continue to exist

Discuss These Quotes from the Novel,
The Black Album[1] with a Partner

1. Chad: "There's a bit of Hitler in all white people [...]"   p. 12

2. Shahid: "He's [Prince] half black and white, half man, half woman, half size, feminine, but macho[2], too. His work contains and extends the history of black American music [...] He can play soul and funk and rock and rap –"   p. 25

3. Chad: "But we must not assimilate, that way we lose our souls. We are proud and we are obedient."   p. 81

4. The problem was, when he [Shahid] was with his friends their story compelled[3] him. But when he walked out, like someone leaving a cinema, he found the world to be more subtle and inexplicable. He knew, too, that stories were made up by men and women; they could not be true or false, for they were exercises in that most magnificent but unreliable capacity, the imagination, which William Blake[4] called "the divine[5] body in every man."   p. 133

5. Like pornography, religion couldn't admit the comic.   p. 150

6. Riaz: "You see, all fiction is, by its very nature, a form of lying – a perversion of truth. Isn't the phrase 'telling stories' used when children tell lies? [...]"   p. 182

7. "A free imagination," Shahid said, "ranges over[6] many natures. A free imagination, looking into itself, illuminates[7] others."   p. 183

---

[1] **The Black Album**, Faber and Faber Ltd, London, 1995
[2] macho ['mætʃəʊ] (Spanish): demonstrating one's masculinity
[3] to compel: (here): to overpower
[4] William Blake (1757–1827): English poet, painter, and engraver
[5] divine: godlike
[6] to range over: to wander about an area
[7] to illuminate: (here): to provide s.o. with insights

8. Deedee: "What sort of people burn books and read aubergines? I'd heard books were on the way out. I never imagined they'd be replaced by vegetables. Presumably[8], libraries will be replaced by greengrocers. [...]"

p. 210

9. How could anyone confine[9] themselves to one system or creed[10]? Why should they feel they had to? There was no fixed self; surely our several selves melted and mutated daily. There had to be innumerable[11] ways of being in the world. He [Shahid] would spread himself out, in his work and in love, following his curiosity.

p. 274

---

[8] presumably: one can suppose
[9] to confine: to limit
[10] creed: belief
[11] innumerable: countless

Reviews of *The Black Album* (Play, 2009)

The Independent – Michael Coveney   22 July

It lives on the page but it dies on the stage. That, alas[1], is the story of
Hanif Kureishi's second brilliant novel.

The National's[2] co-production with Tara Arts[3] has its heart in the right
place but its judgemental faculties absolutely nowhere.

How can something so absolutely boring and tritely[4] old-fashioned in
presentational terms[5] claim to be widening the NT's remit[6]?

Jatinder Verma's stunningly[7] prosaic[8], badly cast[9] and very badly de-
signed production all looks like a retread[10] of a best forgotten fringe
play[11] of about 1979.

http://www.independent.co.uk/arts-entertainment/theatre-dance/reviews/
first-night-the-black-album-national-theatre-london-1756016.html

Daily Telegraph – Dominic Cavendish   22 July

The Black Album, Hanif Kureishi's new dramatisation of his 1995 novel,
has one ace up its sleeve[12]: it's about a subject that matters – the rise of
radical Islam in the UK.

Episodic in nature, the show can't disguise[13] its origins as a novel. Would
it work better on TV? Yes. Should it have come to the stage, and the
National of all places? Absolutely.

---

[1] alas (old-fashioned): unfortunately
[2] The National: The Royal National Theatre in London, funded in part by the Arts
Council England
[3] Tara Arts: theatre in London that often performs plays by minority groups
[4] tritely: in a dull manner, not in an original way
[5] in presentational terms: considering the means used to present the play on the
stage
[6] remit: remittance, money earned
[7] stunningly: in a manner that surprises
[8] prosaic: (here): very ordinary
[9] badly cast: with the wrong actors for the parts
[10] retread (fig.): remake
[11] fringe play: a play performed at one of the many small theatres in London
[12] an acc up your sleeve (fig.): a secret advantage that can be used at the right moment
[13] to disguise [dɪsˈgaɪz]: to hide

The UK terror threat may just have gone from "severe[14]" to "substantial", but that's no reason to be complacent. This is a long-overdue look at a very urgent issue.

http://www.telegraph.co.uk/culture/theatre/theatre-reviews/5886546/The-Black-Album-at-the-National-Theatre-review.html

The Times – Dominic Maxwell   22 July

Hanif Kureishi's story about an Asian student from Kent choosing between Western liberalism and Muslim fundamentalism has only grown more pertinent[15].
The novel is still worth reading, but Kureishi's stage adaptation is really pretty poor.
The sense of time and place that made the book compulsive[16] has all but vanished here.
Only in a concluding set-piece[17], which links these events to the 7/7 bombings, does the evening take brief theatrical flight.

http://entertainment.timesonline.co.uk/tol/arts_and_entertainment/stage/theatre/article6722689.ece

The Guardian – Michael Billington   22 July

This is a busy, hectic affair that raises all kinds of issues about religious and political faith, *fatwas* and censorship and the purpose of art.
But, as so often with adaptations, you get the bones without the thickness of texture that was part of the original's charm.
The stage version does scant justice to[18] the book's panoramic portrait of late-1980s London with its pubs, clubs and ecstasy-filled raves.
In a nutshell[19], one misses the heady[20] exuberance[21] of Kureishi's descriptive writing.

http://www.guardian.co.uk/stage/2009/jul/22/black-album-review

---

[14] severe: very serious
[15] pertinent: relevant
[16] compulsive: interesting and exciting
[17] set-piece: separate part of a play or literary work that seeks to have an impressive effect
[18] to do scant justice to s.th. : to hardly take s.th. into account
[19] in a nutshell: in a few words
[20] heady: extremely exciting
[21] exuberance: vitality

Evening Standard – Fiona Mountford   22 July

In belatedly[22] adapting his superb 1995 novel for the stage, Hanif Kureishi has done neither himself nor his subject matter many favours.
What was promised as a trenchant[23] exploration of the roots of Islamic fundamentalism in our post-7/7 world ends up as a listless[24] trudge[25] through a series of tired scenes.
Jatinder Verma's uninspired direction has the action shoehorned[26] into a narrow set bounded[27] by screens of video projections.
He's not helped by the fact that Kureishi has failed to translate the comic astringency[28] of his prose, and to bring the supporting characters to anything like fully realised life.

http://www.thisislondon.co.uk/theatre/review-23722662-fundamentalism-lacks-real-depth-in-the-black-album.do

Editorial Guardian   27 July

First, the blunt[29] truth: Hanif Kureishi's new play at the National Theatre, *The Black Album*, is not his best work. But in its failings it also reminds us of where he is strongest. For all his grounding[30] in drama, and all those dread[31] critical adjectives ("vivid", "vibrant", "raucous[32]" – often delivered with just a hint of condescension[33]), Kureishi is a brilliant writer, with a firm commitment[34] to the literary novel. *The Black Album* illustrates that very well: it is a play adapted from Kureishi's 1995 novel of the same name – and yet despite the twin bombardments of stage lighting

---

[22] belatedly: happening later than it should
[23] trenchant: keen or incisive
[24] listless: lacking energy
[25] trudge: a long, tiring walk
[26] to shoehorn (fig.): to stuff into a small space
[27] to bound: to limit
[28] astringency: the quality of being very clever with a minimum of words
[29] blunt: very direct
[30] grounding: training
[31] dread: greatly feared
[32] raucous: loud and rough
[33] condescension: arrogant attitude
[34] commitment: *Engagement*

and loud generic[35] dance music, it cannot convey[36] the headiness[37] of a drug-fuelled rave as effectively as the book's exuberant[38] prose.

http://www.guardian.co.uk/commentisfree/2009/jul/27/
hanif-kureishi-drama-novels

The Times – John Lewis   27 July

The Black Album dramatises much of these leftwing apologies for fundamentalism. It features[39] a Marxist academic, distraught[40] by the collapse of the Soviet Union, who instead embraces identity politics and seeks a revolutionary alliance with Islamic militants. There is also a Labour council leader who expediently panders to[41] Islamic fundamentalists. Both have shades[42] of George Galloway[43] about them.

http://entertainment.timesonline.co.uk/tol/arts_and_entertainment/stage/theatre/
article6583407.ece

---

[35] generic: (here): of a particular style
[36] to convey: to bring across
[37] headiness: excitement
[38] exuberant: lively
[39] to feature: to include as a main characteristic
[40] distraught: greatly upset
[41] to pander to: to try to please s.o. so as to get this person's support
[42] shade: (here): hint
[43] George Galloway (1954): British politician who was a Member of Parliament from 1987 to 2010. He was an MP for the Labour Party until his expulsion from the party in 2003. In addition to being opposed to the Iraq War, he then became a founding member of the left-wing Respect Party.

Suggested Additional Reading

1. **The Black Album** (novel) by Hanif Kureishi, Faber and Faber, London, 1995

2. *My Son the Fanatic* (short story) by Hanif Kureishi in **The Many Voices of English**, Diesterweg, Braunschweig, 2005

A film version is available as a DVD in the USA.

3. **1984** by George Orwell, Penguin, Harmondworth, England, 2008

There are two film versions.

4. **Fahrenheit 451** by Ray Bradbury, Diesterweg, Braunschweig, 2008

There is one film version.

5. **Brave New World** by Aldous Huxley, Diesterweg, Braunschweig, 2010

Glossary

Allegory: a narrative in verse or prose in which specific characters and actions represent abstract ideas or moral qualities – An allegory can be literal, or real, and have symbolic levels of meaning.

Alliteration: the repetition of consonant or vowel sounds at the beginning of words

Allusion: a reference to a person, place, event, or written work such as the Bible that the author expects the reader to recognise

Anaphora: the repetition of the same word or words at the beginning of successive phrases, clauses, or sentences

Antagonist: the character or force that opposes the protagonist or hero in a conflict

Archaism: a word or expression that is out of date

Argumentation: writing or a speech that tries to convince the reader of the logic and merits of a particular viewpoint by giving specific reasons and examples

Aside: when an actor/actress speaks directly to the audience and not to the other characters

Audience: people who watch a play

Cast: the actors/actresses in a play

Cast of Characters: the characters in a play

Characterisation: the means used by the author to develop the character, e.g. by description, what the character thinks or says, how he/she reacts or speaks, and how the other characters react or describe the character – The character may be superficially described or flat, or made to seem very real and complex: round.

Climax: the turning point of the story or a play, the crisis, after which there seems to be no other possible way for the plot to continue – The part of the plot before the climax is often called **rising action** and that after the climax **falling action.**

Comedy: in the classical drama: when the hero overcomes his difficulties, or any play that seeks to amuse

Commentary: The author inserts his or her own comments or views.

Complication: the point in the story at which the conflict is introduced, thus giving the plot a new impetus

Conflict: the clash between opposing forces – It can involve ideas, persons, the forces of nature and be in the mind or external.

Dénouement: the part of a story or play when all questions are answered, secrets are revealed, conflicts are resolved, also called **resolution** or **outcome**

Description: The playwright describes the characters as they should appear on the stage.

Dialogue: the actors talking with each other

Diction: the choice of words used by the playwright to produce a certain effect

Director: person who supervises the production of a play

Doppelgänger: a duplicate of a character, often of a mysterious or ghostly nature

Dramatic Irony: when a character says something without realising the true significance of what was said, however, it is obvious to the audience

Euphemism: the substitution of a mild or less negative word or phrase for a direct one, as in the use of "to pass away" instead of "to die"

Exposition: the part of a story or play, usually at the beginning, that gives essential background information for an understanding of the unfolding plot

Farce: comedy, usually about something ridiculous, often with stock characters

Fairy Tale: magical story for children (*Märchen*)

Flashback: a scene in a story or play that interrupts the action to show what happened in the past

Foil: character who is the opposite of another character in order to point up the strengths or weaknesses of the other character

Footlights: small lights at the front edge of a stage

Foreshadowing: a hint that something, usually bad, is going to happen later

Hyperbole: an exaggeration

Irony: when a character means the opposite of what he/she actually writes or says

Lighting: the use of electric lights to create a certain atmosphere, from various positions around the stage, also with spotlights

Metaphor: a direct comparison between two apparently different things, ideas, or persons without using *as* or *like*, i.e. She had rose lips.

Monologue: when an actor/actress speaks alone on the stage

Motivation: the force that drives a character to take a certain course of action

Mood: overall atmosphere of a work

Offstage: away from the acting area

The Other: a concept that has its origin in psychology – It describes the tendency of a dominant group to look upon different cultural or religious groups as strange and different, even inferior. For example, British colonisers often considered indigenous people under their control, in Africa, India, Australia, or New Zealand, as barbarous and uncivilised. They needed to be brought to the level of Western education and morals. **Othering** is the process of putting the stamp of **the other** on a person or persons.

Oxymoron: the combining of two terms that contradict each other, e.g. a cold fire

To Learn a Part: to learn the lines of a character in the play by heart

Paradox: a statement that seems to be contradictory

Polysydeton: a rhetorical device whereby a conjunction, often *and*, is used repeatedly – frequently used in the Bible

Plot: the plan and arrangement of related incidents within a story or play

Prompter: person at the front of the stage who whispers the lines of a play that an actor/actress forgets

Prop: any movable property used on the set of a stage play

Protagonist: the main character in a story on whom the action centres

Rehearsal: a session of practising a play

Register: the kind of language used in a specific social setting – Examples of register are slang, colloquial, and formal. The kind of register used often reflects the social status of the character or may be purposely used in the wrong context or setting.

Repetition: repeating a word or phrase in a sentence to produce an effect

Sarcasm: the use of ironic remarks to show you dislike s.o.

Satire: the use of sarcasm or irony to show the moral weakness of people, an idea, a movement, a country, etc.

Scenery: the painted backcloths, stage structures, etc., used to represent a location

Script: the text of a play

Set: scenery and props to determine a certain location

Simile: a direct comparison between two basically different things, ideas, or persons using *as* or *like*, i.e. She had lips like a rose.

Stock Character or Stereotype: a character with typical characteristics who keeps reappearing in literature, such as the jealous husband, the all-knowing but silent butler, the absent-minded professor, the hypocritical preacher

Stage Curtains: the main curtains that open and close at the front of the stage

Stage Directions: instructions to an actor/actress or director in the script

Suspense: the feeling of uncertainty and anxiety as the plot rises towards its climax

Symbol: anything that has a meaning in itself, but also stands for something larger than itself

Topos, plural **Topoi:** a traditional theme or motif, such as the jealous husband, young lovers, good overcoming evil, the servant of several masters (picaroon) who is able to trick them all, the beautiful woman who bewitches all men, the mad scientist, the devil buying souls

Tragedy: in the classical drama: a person of importance who falls to disaster because of a personal failing (fatal flaw), or any play that ends in a disaster

Understudy: actor/actress who learns a part in a play so as to be ready to replace an actor/actress at a moment's notice

Upstage: part of the stage at the back

Wing: the space offstage to the left and right of the acting area